SMALL ARMS

17th CENTURY TO THE PRESENT DAY

SMALL ARMS
17th CENTURY TO THE PRESENT DAY

FEATURES SEVEN VIEWS OF EACH SMALL ARM

MARTIN J. DOUGHERTY
ILLUSTRATIONS BY
COLIN PEARSON

amber
BOOKS

This edition first published in 2011

Published by
Amber Books Ltd
Bradley's Close
74–77 White Lion Street
London N1 9PF
United Kingdom
www.amberbooks.co.uk

ISBN: 978-1-907446-80-1

Printed in China

Project Editor: Sarah Uttridge
Designer: Zoë Mellors
Picture Research: Terry Forshaw

Digital illustrations courtesy of Military Visualizations, Inc.

Contents

Introduction 6

Creating the Digital Models 10

Dog Lock Pistol 12

Pepperbox .45 18

Luger (p'08) 24

Colt M1911 30

Smith & Wesson M29 36

Automag 180 42

SIG-Sauer P226 48

Beretta 93R (Raffica) 54

Smith & Wesson 4506 60

MP38 66

Thompson M1928 72

Sten Mk II 78

Uzi 84

MP5K 90

Tec9 (TEC-DC9) 96

Lee-Enfield 102

KAR-98 108

Winchester M70 114

Martini-Henry 120

MP44/StG44 126

AK47 132

M16A1/A2 138

Dragunov 144

M82/M107 Barrett 150

M4A1 156

Lewis Gun 162

Browning .30 cal 168

M2 .50 cal 174

Bren MG 180

MG42 186

M60 192

Bazooka 198

Panzerfaust 204

RPG-7 210

Stinger 216

Index 222

Introduction

The term 'small arms' probably originated in the earliest years of firearm use, to differentiate gunpowder weapons carried by individual personnel from artillery guns. Today's small arms can be divided into three broad categories: sidearms, combat weapons and support weapons.

No firearm can excel in all roles. Different applications may require entirely different characteristics. Thus a weapon that is excellent for close-quarters battle in urban terrain is likely to be less useful at long distances over open ground.

Among the most important factors for any weapon is 'stopping power'. This is the ability of the weapon to disable an opponent and prevent him from doing whatever he was intent on at the moment he was hit. Stopping power is more important than lethality in combat; an enemy who is immediately downed has less chance to inflict casualties than one who takes time to succumb to his wounds.

.44 SMITH & WESSON

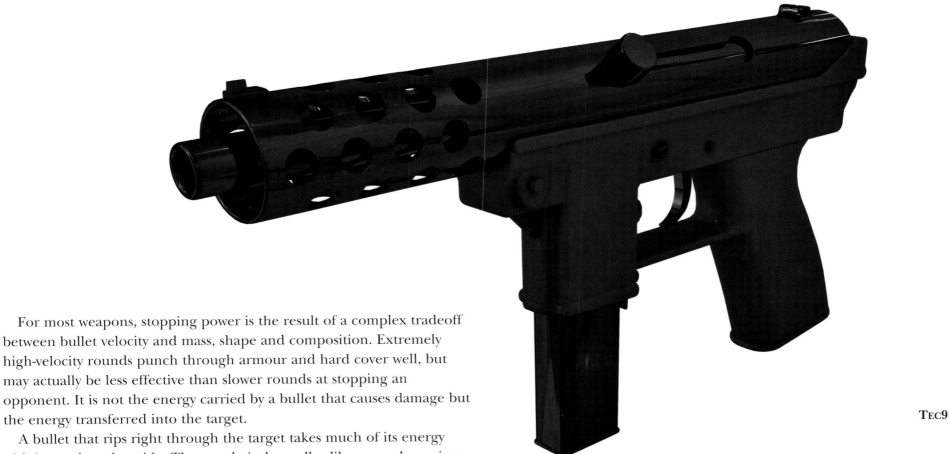

For most weapons, stopping power is the result of a complex tradeoff between bullet velocity and mass, shape and composition. Extremely high-velocity rounds punch through armour and hard cover well, but may actually be less effective than slower rounds at stopping an opponent. It is not the energy carried by a bullet that causes damage but the energy transferred into the target.

A bullet that rips right through the target takes much of its energy with it out the other side. Thus a relatively small-calibre round, moving very fast, will penetrate body armour well but can also pose a hazard to non-combatants and friendlies through over-penetration and ricochets. A lower-velocity round might actually be more effective against unarmoured targets, though any bullet can kill instantly if it hits a vital organ.

Accuracy of the gun

High velocity also contributes to accuracy. Bullets travel in a ballistic arc rather than a straight line, and are affected by wind. These effects are negligible over short distances, but as range increases the velocity of the projectile becomes more significant. Accuracy is also affected by factors such as the length of the weapon's barrel and the quality of its construction. When choosing the most effective weapon for a given task, it is necessary to balance accuracy and stopping power against other factors such as rate of fire, ammunition capacity and ease of carry. Recoil

Tec9

characteristics are also important; there is no point in carrying an immensely powerful weapon around if it is uncontrollable; hitting the target with anything is more effective than missing with the most potent weapon on the planet.

Small arm categories

There is considerable variety among small arms, but they can be divided into three categories: sidearms, combat weapons and support weapons. Sidearms are primarily carried for self-defence or as a backup weapon, though they can also be a status symbol or a tool with which to enforce discipline. The most common military sidearms are semi-automatic handguns, though sometimes revolvers or small submachineguns are used instead.

Combat weapons include submachineguns, rifles and carbines. These are the weapons that will equip most members of an infantry squad, and provide the majority of the unit's fighting power. Which weapons are selected depends on the environment in which the force expects to fight.

Submachineguns are very effective in urban combat, where ranges tend to be short. Their high rate of fire enables a target to be quickly disabled, while the small size of the weapon is handy when manoeuvring in confined spaces. They fire a pistol cartridge, which limits their range and ability to penetrate hard cover or body armour. However, the lightness and small size of their ammuition enables a large number to be carried in a magazine.

Submachineguns fall into two general types. The first has much in common with an overgrown handgun, and is fed from a magazine inserted through the handgrip. These pistol-type SMGs are easy to carry and can sometimes be used as a substitute for a handgun. Larger submachineguns are configured more like a rifle and are heavier but somewhat more accurate than their smaller brethren.

Rifles and carbines are the commonest personal weapons carried by infantry soldiers. Generally speaking, the term rifle is applied to a full-sized longarm with a rifled barrel, whilst a smaller, lighter version would be termed a carbine. However, there is much debate about exactly where a lightweight assault rifle becomes a carbine.

WINCHESTER M70

The modern assault rifle is a versatile general-purpose combat weapon. It is accurate to a distance greater than most users can shoot effectively, carries a reasonable amount of ammunition and has good stopping power. Assault rifles are effective at most likely combat ranges and can be switched from fully automatic to more accurate semi-automatic fire where accuracy is more important than firepower.

Support weapons are heavier than typical infantry weapons, though some are light enough to be integrated into a squad. These include light and general-purpose machineguns. Heavier support weapons, such as heavy machineguns, are still very much infantry equipment as opposed to artillery weapons, but are too heavy to be operated or moved by a single individual.

Support weapons also include a range of light explosive weapons intended for attacking tanks, aircraft and enemy strongpoints. Many such weapons consist of a reusable launcher and a single-shot rocket or rocket-propelled grenade, though some are intended to be fired once and then thrown away.

Equipping an infantry force

Using this array of weaponry, it is possible to equip an infantry force to deal with a range of threats and environments. Typically a squad will consist of troops armed with assault rifles or carbines, with a machinegun for fire support and some kind of anti-armour weapon such as a rocket-propelled grenade launcher. Snipers, heavy machineguns and the like will be available for support but tend not to be integrated into a squad. Instead they are deployed separately where their unique capabilities can be best employed.

Creating the Digital Models

Every weapon in this book was originally created as a complex 3D object using computer graphics software commonly employed in the production of movies and video games. From the 3D model, each of the seven-view images was generated, or rendered, from various viewpoints around the model (above, below, and so on). The result is a set of highly detailed 2D images suitable for printing.

1 All 3D objects start with a single point, called a vertex. Its position in the virtual 'space' in the graphics program can be defined by three parameters: X, Y and Z or, in more basic terms, left and right, up and down and back and forth.

2 Once you have three vertices, they can be joined to form a 2D triangle in 3D space, called an edged face.

3 To begin creating a gun barrel, for example, the computer graphics program 'lathes' hundreds of 2D shapes in the Z axis, drawing a barrel shape in three dimensions around the X axis. Every point is defined by different values for X and Y.

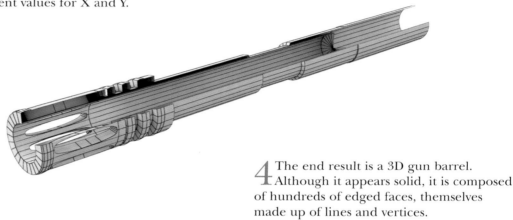

4 The end result is a 3D gun barrel. Although it appears solid, it is composed of hundreds of edged faces, themselves made up of lines and vertices.

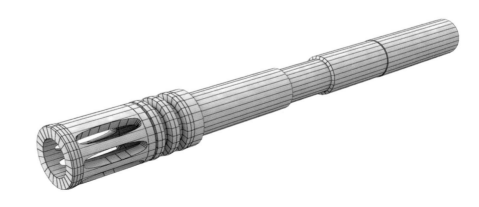

5 To create more complex objects, simple elements are fitted together to form an assembly like the barrel of this M4A1.

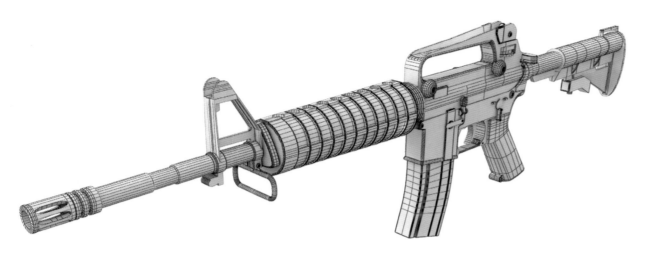

6 A texture is applied to the finished gun to give the appearance of painted steel. Texture is applied by wrapping a stored 2D texture around a 3D object. The finished 3D gun can be textured, painted and lit. Finally it can be rendered from any angle.

7 The finished weapon models on the following pages are all constructed of many hundreds and thousands of individual edged faces, rendered and textured from different angles. This is a model of the M4A1.

Dog Lock Pistol

Early small arms were fired by touching the glowing end of a slow-match to a pinch of gunpowder held in a pan on the side of the weapon. This in turn initiated the main powder charge via a hole in the side of the weapon. The matchlock system worked well enough to revolutionize warfare, but it did have severe limitations. Various other forms of firing system, or lock, were invented. These dispensed with the match and replaced it with a mechanical device that struck sparks using a flint. This eliminated the need to keep a slow-match burning under combat conditions. The dog lock was one of several forms of flintlock mechanism. Although clumsy by modern standards, dog lock weapons enabled the user to carry a weapon ready to fire for some time, and were fairly reliable in action. Virtually all weapons of this era were smoothbores – i.e. they fired a somewhat loose-fitting ball from an unrifled barrel. As a result, even long guns were extremely inaccurate, and the heavy ball quickly lost velocity as it passed through the air. Pistols suffered from an even shorter accurate range. However, a large-calibre dog lock handgun hit hard at close range, and would stop most assailants from outside the reach of a sword. These weapons were often carried by gentlemen for self-defence or by cavalry troopers, who might use them to perform close-range ride-by shootings of enemy personnel before either retiring to reload or charging home with the sword.

SPECIFICATIONS

COUNTRY OF ORIGIN:	United Kingdom
DATE:	1650–1680
CALIBRE:	10.9mm (.42in)
OPERATION:	Flintlock
WEIGHT:	1.02kg (2lb 4oz)
OVERALL LENGTH:	394mm (15.5in)
BARREL LENGTH:	292mm (11.5in)
MUZZLE VELOCITY:	122m/s (400ft/s)
FEED:	Single shot

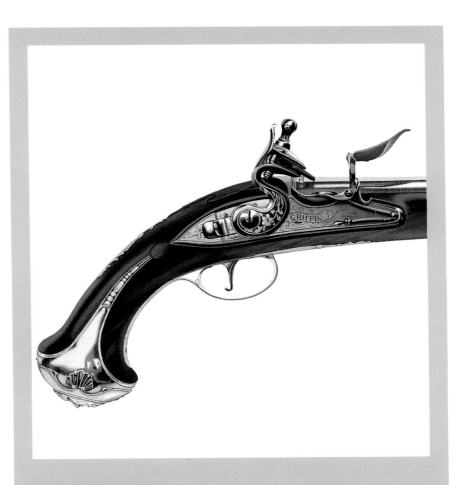

DOG LOCK PISTOL FACTS:

- Smoothbore single-shot flintlock pistol
- Long reloading time
- Extremely short effective range

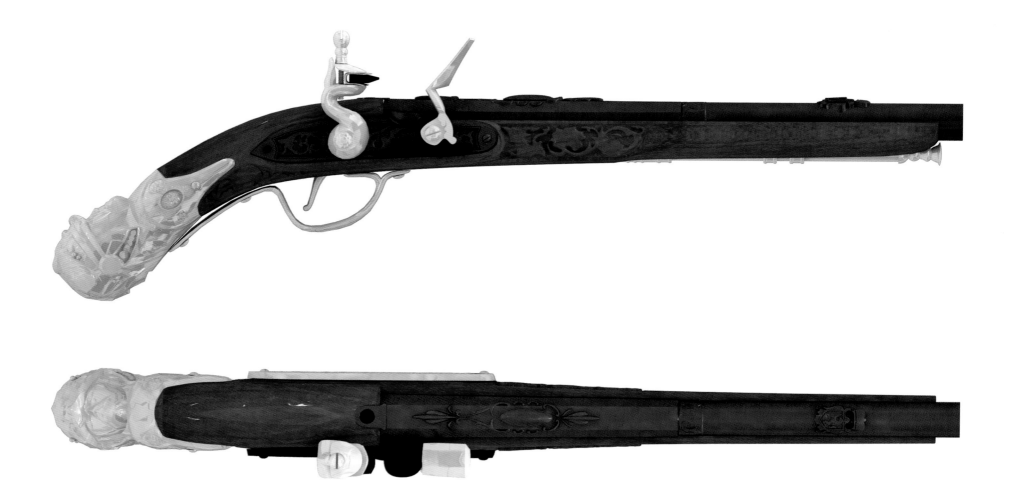

The weapon could be left uncocked and therefore safe. The spring-loaded lock was manually pulled back to the cocked position and remained there until released by the trigger, at which point the lock fell forward to initiate firing. The hammer of a modern handgun works in a remarkably similar manner.

A dog lock weapon was loaded by pouring loose gunpowder down the barrel, then adding a ball and a paper wad to hold it all in place. Additional powder in the pan primed the weapon, ready to fire.

AN ARM EXTENSION

A good pistol was a point-and-shoot weapon, functioning like an extension of the user's arm. Sights were largely irrelevant; at any range where they might be useful, the inherent inaccuracy of the weapon made them less than useful. At short range the most effective use of a pistol was to point it as if pointing a finger. Even then, the 'lock time' between pulling the trigger and the weapon discharging was variable, requiring the weapon to be held on target throughout. It was not uncommon for priming powder to 'flash in the pan' without igniting the main charge, thus causing a misfire, or to 'hang-fire' for a few seconds and then discharge. This could mean the shot came too late to save the user, or cause an unintended casualty.

Pepperbox .45

The chief drawbacks of flintlock weapons were their poor reliability and long reloading time. The former was largely overcome by the introduction of the percussion cap. This device allowed the flint to be replaced with a hammer, and the unreliable priming-pan and touchhole setup to be done away with. Instead of striking sparks into the pan, the weapon's lock dropped the hammer onto a percussion cap, which then detonated and initiated the main propellant charge. The latter was little different to that of a flintlock weapon, but at least firing was more reliable. Reloading times were still long, so to overcome this a range of multi-barrel weapons were introduced. The most common of these were 'pepperbox' weapons, so named for their resemblance to a pepper grinder. Pepperbox weapons had several individually loaded barrels, which could be rotated in turn to line up with the firing mechanism. Early pepperbox weapons used manual rotation and a flintlock system, but the definitive pepperbox was a percussion-cap weapon whose barrels were rotated by the early stage of trigger pull. This also cocked the hammer; completing the trigger pull dropped the hammer and fired the weapon. Mechanical pepperbox pistols were still slow to load, but could carry several rounds ready for use, thus greatly increasing firepower. Perhaps more importantly, the weapon was small enough to carry conveniently in a pocket and could be fired with confidence immediately after being brought into action.

SPECIFICATIONS

COUNTRY OF ORIGIN:	United States
DATE:	1830s
CALIBRE:	11.4mm (.45in)
OPERATION:	Percussion Cap
WEIGHT:	0.42kg (15oz)
OVERALL LENGTH:	279mm (11in)
BARREL LENGTH:	127mm (5in)
MUZZLE VELOCITY:	168mps (550fps)
FEED:	One per barrel

PEPPERBOX .45 FACTS:

- .45 calibre percussion-cap pistol
- Smoothbore and rifled-barrel versions
- Potential for multiple accidental discharge

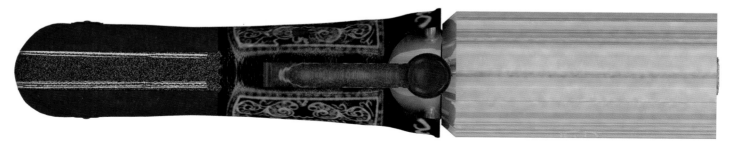

The pepperbox pistol was in many ways the forerunner of the modern revolver, though instead of a rotating cylinder, each barrel was presented in turn. This made the mounting of sights problematical.

A malfunction known as a 'chain-fire' could cause all loaded barrels to be initiated by firing a shot. Whilst hazardous, this was less serious than in an early revolver, as each round had a clear path out of the weapon, which was thus far less likely to explode in the user's hand.

RELIABLE BUT CLUMSY

Although clumsy by modern standards, a well-made pepperbox pistol offered compact, reliable firepower. Many were not well made, however, posing a hazard to the user as well as anyone else nearby. If the barrel did not line up properly with the hammer, which was not uncommon with cheap pepperboxes, the weapon might fail to fire. Badly-made cylinders could rupture, igniting the other charges and causing the weapon to explode. Pepperboxes were less prone to hang-fires than flintlocks – i.e. they either did or did not fire rather than discharging a few seconds after the trigger was pulled. And whereas a flintlock that failed was useless, a pepperbox user could attempt to shoot with the next barrel in sequence.

Luger (P '08)

The 'Luger' pistol is known by various designations, including Parabellum '08 (or P '08) and Pistole 1928. Its origins date back to a 7.65mm (0.3in) calibre weapon created in 1893 by Hugo Borchardt. This handgun was in use with the Swiss army in 1900, at which time George Luger created an improved version. Luger's handgun was chambered for the 9mm (0.35in) Parabellum cartridge, and went into production as a sidearm for the German armed forces. By the outbreak of World War I, the standard Luger was available in large numbers, with variant models becoming available. These included the 'Long '08' pistol, which was used by the German navy as well as troops whose primary duty was not direct infantry combat with the enemy, such as engineers and artillerymen. In theory, attaching the weapon's rigid holster to the handgrip allowed it to function as a carbine. This did not prove effective in practice, however. A 32-round 'snail drum' magazine could be used with the long or standard P '08 for increased firepower. However, the large magazines were unreliable and did not share the Luger's remarkable longevity. Despite a fairly complex set of internal workings, the Luger proved reliable and popular with its users. It was a highly 'pointable' weapon and comfortable to shoot, contributing to effectiveness in close-quarters combat. Thus whilst the long-range version failed to be an effective substitute for a proper longarm, the handgun version became a massive success, with over two million manufactured.

SPECIFICATIONS

COUNTRY OF ORIGIN:	Germany
DATE:	1908
CALIBRE:	9mm (0.35in) Parabellum
OPERATION:	Short recoil
WEIGHT:	0.876kg (2lb)
OVERALL LENGTH:	222mm (8.74in)
BARREL LENGTH:	103mm (4in)
MUZZLE VELOCITY:	320m/sec (1050ft/sec)
FEED:	Eight-round box magazine

LUGER (P '08) FACTS:

- 9 x 19mm (0.35 x 0.75in) calibre semi-automatic pistol
- Reliable and easy to shoot
- Complex and expensive to manufacture

The P '08 was manufactured in huge numbers in Germany and overseas. Versions were built in Britain and supplied to Dutch forces serving in Southeast Asia. Copies and licensed versions were made in Finland, Portugal and several other nations.

The complexity of the P '08 meant that it was expensive and time-consuming to manufacture. The intent was to replace it in German service with the simpler Walther P38, but this weapon was not available in large numbers by the outbreak of World War II.

A WARTIME WARRIOR

The Luger was originally chambered for 7.65 x 22mm (0.3 x 0.87in) ammunition, a common pistol round at the time. A new round was developed for it, using a 9mm (0.35in) bullet, which proved so successful that it has been one of the standard ammunition calibres for over a century. This new 9 x 19mm (0.35 x 0.75in) Parabellum (or 9mm/0.35in Luger) round was made popular due to the success of the Luger pistol, which served through both world wars and remains a popular target weapon to this day. Although the toggle-lock mechanism could be prone to jamming due to dirt, a well-cared-for Luger was a reliable sidearm even under harsh wartime conditions, and became a popular souvenir from both world wars.

Colt M1911

The Colt M1911 has been in use for nearly a century. It was developed by John Browning and gained its designation from its date of adoption as a sidearm for US forces, who needed a weapon with more stopping power than the .38 Special revolvers then in use. Chambered for .45 ACP (Automatic Colt Pistol) ammunition and fed from a seven-round magazine, the M1911 offered only a slight increase in ammunition capacity over a revolver but was faster to reload and significantly more powerful. The M1911 uses Browning's short-recoil system, which relies on gas pressure in the firing chamber to drive the slide back, ejecting the spent cartridge and feeding a fresh round into the chamber. This system has become standard on a great many handguns and is used on virtually all weapons chambered for 9mm (0.35in) or greater. Experience with early models, notably during World War I, led to the introduction of an improved version, designated M1911A1. The mechanics of the weapon remained unchanged, but it gained a wider ejection port to reduce the chance of an ammunition stoppage and an elongated spur above the grip to reduce the chance of the user's hand being caught by the slide. Although it was finally replaced in the 1990s as the main US military sidearm by the 9mm (0.35in) M9, the M1911 remains popular with law enforcement and specialist military units, as well as with private users who carry a weapon for self-defence.

SPECIFICATIONS

COUNTRY OF ORIGIN:	United States
DATE:	1911
CALIBRE:	11.43mm (0.45in) ACP
OPERATION:	Short recoil
WEIGHT:	1.36kg (3lb)
OVERALL LENGTH:	219mm (8.62in)
BARREL LENGTH:	128mm (5in)
MUZZLE VELOCITY:	252m/sec (825ft/sec)
FEED:	Seven-round box magazine

COLT M1911 FACTS:

- .45 ACP semi-automatic pistol
- Very good stopping power
- Relatively small magazine capacity

Gas pressure in the firing chamber drives both the barrel and the slide, which are locked together for firing, back. A pivoting link disconnects the slide and barrel, allowing the slide to continue backwards. This pushes the hammer back to its cocked position. The slide then runs forward again, picking up a round from the magazine and returning to the locked position.

The M1911 has a grip safety located on the rear of the handgrip. If the weapon is not held properly, the trigger is disconnected. A manual safety on the left side of the frame prevents the weapon from firing at all if it is engaged.

DISABLE THE TARGET

The M1911 has a reassuring heft in the hands. Like all handguns, it is most effective when fired from a good two-handed stance, but this is not always possible in the middle of combat. Most users can control the M1911's recoil one-handed, though its heavy round does cause it to kick fairly hard. The .45 ACP round is prized for its stopping power. It is a relatively low-velocity round, which generally causes it to stop inside the target and transfer all of its kinetic energy, rather than tearing out the back with some of its energy unspent. This reduces the hazard from 'over-penetration' as well as increasing the ability of the round to do its job – which is to disable but not necessarily kill the target.

Smith & Wesson M29

The Smith & Wesson M29 is a heavy-frame double-action revolver chambered for the .44 Magnum cartridge. Magnum cartridges are slightly longer than is standard for ammunition of that calibre, and thus contain more propellant. This translates to a higher muzzle velocity, more stopping power, and heavy recoil. The M29 was made famous in the movies as the world's most powerful handgun. This is not strictly accurate; a number of weapons exist that are actually more potent. However, most of these are fairly uncommon, so the .44 Magnum can claim to be the most powerful among mainstream handguns. Revolvers are 'mechanical repeaters' – i.e. the action of placing a new round under the hammer is carried out by the user and does not depend on the energy generated by firing the weapon. This permits robust construction and a firing chamber that can withstand high pressures. As a result, very powerful cartridges became available for use in revolvers long before semi-automatics that could handle them were developed. A .44 Magnum revolver can fire standard .44 Special cartridges, but not vice versa; the longer rounds will not fit in a 'lesser' weapon. This is just as well, since the chamber pressure could endanger a lighter-framed revolver. The M29 is available with a range of barrel lengths, including a lightweight version with a 101mm (4in) barrel. However, the weight of the weapon serves to absorb some of the recoil, so the shorter-barrel versions might actually be less controllable for lighter shooters.

SPECIFICATIONS

COUNTRY OF ORIGIN:	United States
DATE:	1955
CALIBRE:	.44 Magnum
OPERATION:	Double-action revolver
WEIGHT:	1.46kg (3lb 4oz)
OVERALL LENGTH:	353mm (13.9in)
BARREL LENGTH:	213mm (8.39in)
MUZZLE VELOCITY:	About 376m/sec (1400ft/sec)
FEED:	Six-round cylinder

SMITH & WESSON M29 FACTS:

- .44 Magnum calibre revolver
- Extremely powerful cartridge
- Heavy recoil reduces controllability for some shooters

Early versions of the M29 had a shrouded ejector rod. Later production models have an extended shroud running the length of the barrel. The Model 629 Classic, an updated version, became available in 1979.

The M29 can be fired double-action, with the trigger pull setting the hammer and revolving the cylinder before firing the weapon, or single-action. In the latter case the hammer is thumbcocked and requires a very light trigger pull to release it. This benefits accurate shooting and is also extremely intimidating in a situation where the user wants to deter violence.

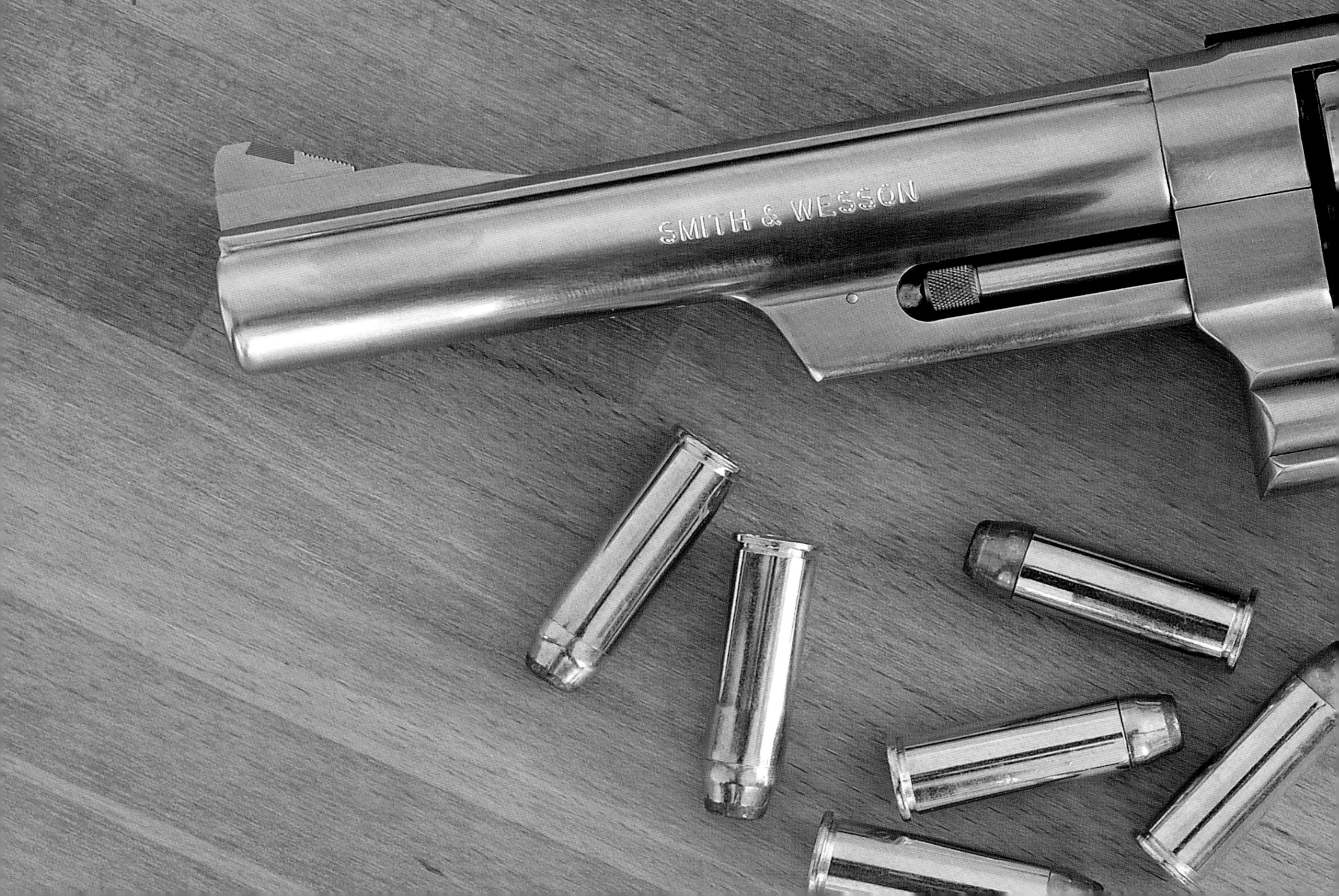
SMITH & WESSON

MAGNUM FLINCH

Firing such powerful rounds requires a thick cylinder wall to avoid ruptures, and a heavy frame to withstand the recoil forces. A weaker weapon might distort over time, potentially leading to malfunction. The recoil of such a potent round can also be hazardous for the user – it is not uncommon for the muzzle to jump up and hit an unwary firer in the face. Obviously, it is impossible to rely on a weapon that you cannot control. However powerful a round might be, it is useless if it misses due to uncontrolled recoil or is not fired because it took the user too long to get the weapon back on target after a miss. The expected kick of handguns can also cause 'Magnum flinch', greatly reducing accuracy.

Automag 180

The Automag, as its name suggests, was developed to shoot the powerful .44 Magnum round from a semi-automatic pistol. This presented significant engineering challenges, not least due to the extreme chamber pressures created by Magnum rounds. After a series of experimental weapons in various calibres, the definitive .44 design was created, but went into production in a less robust and reliable form than had been intended. Nevertheless, the weapon was expensive to produce, and so much money was lost on those made in the original production run (about 3000) that the Automag Corporation went out of business after only a few months. However, the idea of a Magnum-calibre semi-automatic pistol remained attractive, and several copies and developed versions have been produced under a range of names. A number of weapons have been marketed under the Automag name, chambered for ammunition ranging from .22 Winchester Magnum Rimfire to .50 Action Express. The original Automag did not use standard .44 Magnum rounds, but a specially developed cartridge named .44 Automag Pistol (AMP). This was originally created from a cut-down rifle round. A .357 Automag Pistol round followed later, with cartridges in other calibres produced by later manufacturers. The Automag's lack of market success was due more to business decisions than to flaws with the weapon. The new generation of high-power semi-automatics perhaps owes its existence to this iconic but unsuccessful weapon.

SPECIFICATIONS

COUNTRY OF ORIGIN:	United States
DATE:	Produced 1971–1982
CALIBRE:	11mm (0.44in) AMP
OPERATION:	Short recoil
WEIGHT:	1.62kg (3lb 9oz)
OVERALL LENGTH:	292mm (11.5in)
BARREL LENGTH:	165mm (6.49in)
MUZZLE VELOCITY:	442m/sec (1450ft/sec)
FEED:	Seven-round single-column box magazine

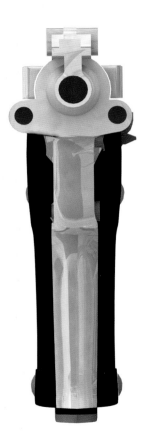

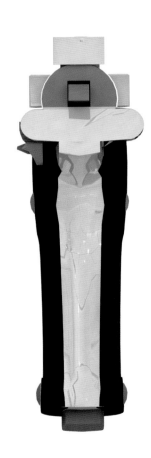

AUTOMAG 180 FACTS:

- .44 Magnum semi-automatic pistol
- Extremely powerful cartridge
- Has returned to production in several guises

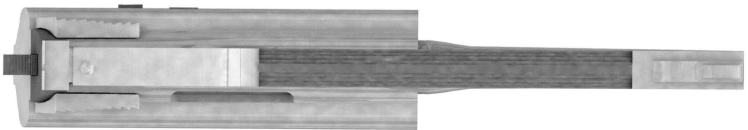

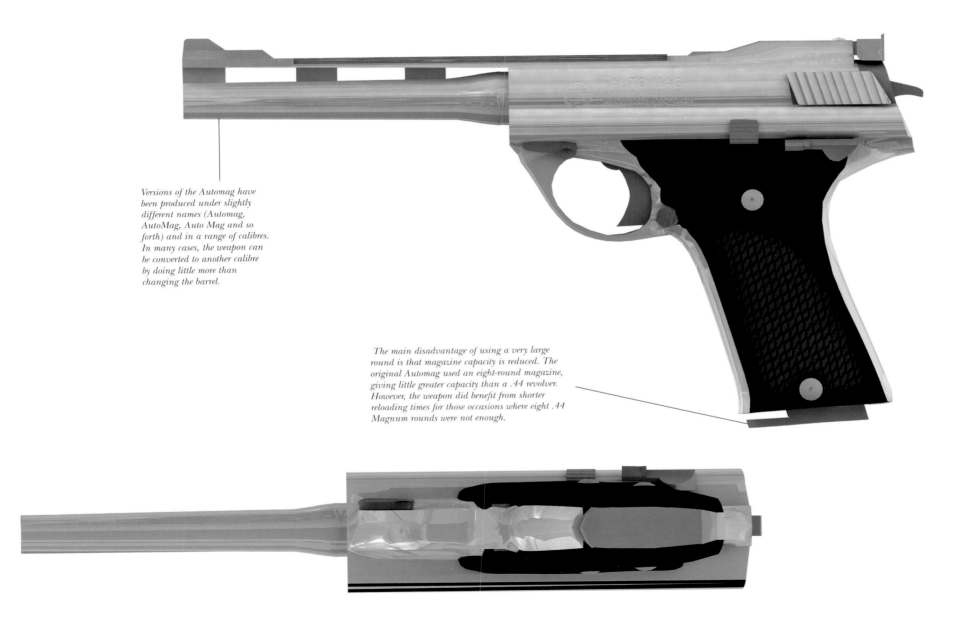

Versions of the Automag have been produced under slightly different names (Automag, AutoMag, Auto Mag and so forth) and in a range of calibres. In many cases, the weapon can be converted to another calibre by doing little more than changing the barrel.

The main disadvantage of using a very large round is that magazine capacity is reduced. The original Automag used an eight-round magazine, giving little greater capacity than a .44 revolver. However, the weapon did benefit from shorter reloading times for those occasions where eight .44 Magnum rounds were not enough.

ROTARY BOLT

The Automag is a weapon whose designers managed to solve most of the problems with an extremely powerful semi-automatic pistol. Whereas a revolver cylinder is locked in place during firing, a semi-automatic action must by definition be able to move, creating the possibility of a serious malfunction. An escape of high-pressure propellant gas could endanger the user, and even less powerful pistols have sometimes thrown the detached slide back into the user's face. In a powerful handgun this would be serious, and thus the Automag had to withstand the chamber pressures generated by its ammunition yet still function correctly. The solution was to use a rotary bolt not dissimilar to that used in assault rifles.

SIG-Sauer P226

The P226 was developed from SIG-Sauer's P220 specifically to compete in trials to find a replacement for the venerable M1911 in US military service. The P226 lost out on cost factors to the Beretta 92, the only other weapon to meet all requirements. However, it has since been adopted by a range of military and law enforcement users who are prepared to pay a higher price for excellence. The P226 is available in 9mm (0.35in), .40 (10mm) and .357 (9.06mm) SIG calibres. The latter is a high-velocity, high-penetration round favoured by some US law enforcement and security agencies. The staggered-column magazine holds more ammunition than the P220 – typically 15 rounds for a 9mm (0.35in) model, though other magazine sizes are available. Like most other large-calibre semi-automatics, the P-226 uses the short-recoil system developed over a century ago by John Browning. However, this has been modified with the use of an enlarged breech section to lock barrel and slide together, rather than the original locking lugs. This system was developed by SIG and has been widely adopted by other manufacturers. Most P226 pistols have a double-action trigger and a decocking lever rather than a conventional safety. A round is chambered from the magazine, and the hammer then decocked. The firing pin is locked except during the final stage of trigger movement. The weapon can be carried safely with a round chambered, and brought instantly into action by simply pulling the trigger.

SPECIFICATIONS

COUNTRY OF ORIGIN:	Switzerland
DATE:	1981
CALIBRE:	9mm (0.35in) Parabellum
OPERATION:	Short recoil
WEIGHT:	0.75kg (1lb 10oz)
OVERALL LENGTH:	196mm (7.7in)
BARREL LENGTH:	112mm (4.4in)
MUZZLE VELOCITY:	426m/sec (1400ft/sec)
FEED:	15-round box magazine

SIG-SAUER P226 FACTS:

- High capacity semi-automatic pistol
- Double-action with no manual safety
- More expensive than many competitors

The current standard P226 is the P226 Rail variant, which has a Picatinny rail under the barrel for the attachment of accessories such as a tactical light.

The user can choose to manually cock the weapon before firing, or can bring it into action quickly by using double-action to set the hammer and then drop it. Slide movement from the first shot recocks the hammer for further single-action fire.

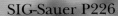

IMPRESSIVE FEATURES

The P226 is not cheap but it is well made with excellent features. Although it uses a double-stacked magazine, it is not excessively wide, and it is very compact for a high-capacity 9mm (0.35in) pistol. High-visibility sights are fitted as standard, and the pistol makes good use of them. Only the P226 and the Beretta 92 handguns met or exceeded all the requirements of the infamous US Army pistol trials. The Beretta was cheaper and was ultimately selected; cost is important when the huge numbers required by a superpower's armed forces are considered. However, the P226 remains popular with specialist units, private users and law enforcement agencies, which buy weapons in smaller numbers.

Beretta 93R (Raffica)

The 93R was developed from the more conventional Beretta 92, and shares many components. Where the 92 is a semi-automatic pistol, the 93R is capable of firing three-round bursts. Unlike the 92, the 93R fires single-action only, so has to be manually cocked before firing the first shot. The main external differences between the 93R and the semi-automatic 92 are an extended barrel, sometimes with a muzzle brake to reduce recoil, and the elongated trigger guard with folding foregrip. This enables the firer to steady the weapon better than with a conventional two-handed pistol-shooting grip. However, as with all small automatic weapons, muzzle climb is still a problem. The 93R can use the same magazines as the semi-automatic Beretta 92, but these are soon exhausted. A 20-round extension magazine is available, which extends beyond the handgrip. This can make carrying the weapon in a holster awkward; some users prefer a standard 'carry' magazine with extension magazines available for reloading. Beretta created the 93R with police and bodyguard use in mind, providing high firepower in a small package that can be carried discreetly. In the hands of a skilled shooter it is effective, but accuracy is always a problem when firing a small automatic weapon. A detachable shoulder stock is available, but once this is attached the weapon loses its main advantage of small size. The stock may assist controllability under burst fire, and in theory could allow accurate semi-automatic fire at greater ranges than are attainable with conventional handguns.

SPECIFICATIONS

COUNTRY OF ORIGIN:	*Italy*
DATE:	*1986*
CALIBRE:	*9mm (0.35in) Parabellum*
OPERATION:	*Short recoil*
WEIGHT:	*1.12kg (2lb 8oz)*
OVERALL LENGTH:	*240mm (9.45in)*
BARREL LENGTH:	*156mm (6in)*
MUZZLE VELOCITY:	*375m/sec (1230ft/sec)*
FEED:	*15- or 20-round box magazine*

BERETTA 93R (RAFFICA) FACTS:

- 9 x 19mm (0.35 x 0.75in) burst-capable automatic pistol
- Fires three-round bursts at 1100 RPM
- Hard to control under burst fire

Burst capability offers a compromise between increasing firepower and wasting ammunition. A fully automatic weapon with such a high rate of fire would likely empty itself into the sky before the user could bring it under control.

The 'R' stands for Raffica, which is Italian for 'burst'. The selector switch for burst or semi-automatic mode is located on the same axis as the safety, with the selector pointing forward and the safety rearwards.

A TWO-GRIP PISTOL

It is easy to dismiss a weapon like this as a gimmick more likely to appeal to video gamers than security professionals, but burst-capable pistols are used by many security agencies and bodyguards. The main advantage is portability; nobody would choose to become involved in a firefight armed with an overgrown pistol, but the additional firepower may be the decisive factor in a situation where larger weapons cannot be carried. The foregrip, tiny as it is, helps control the weapon by enabling the user to exert more leverage on the weapon, preventing muzzle climb. A conventional two-handed grip on the butt of the pistol places both hands behind the axis of rotation and is less effective.

Beretta 93R (Raffica)

Smith & Wesson 4506

Smith & Wesson's third generation of semi-automatic handguns are differentiated by a four-digit code. The first two digits indicate calibre, the third is for the frame size and action type, and the fourth is assigned to the weapon's construction. In this case, 4506 indicates a .45-ACP calibre weapon, with a standard frame, double-action trigger and stainless steel construction. Smith & Wesson produce a range of very similar weapons with slightly different characteristics such as calibre, compact or full-sized frames, double-action or double-action-only models, and so forth. Considerable variety is available from what is essentially the same basic weapon. Despite the range of ammunition types available today, many shooters still consider the .45 ACP round to be the absolute last word in stopping power, and will not consider carrying a weapon in any other calibre. The 4506 carries this proven round in a modern handgun that is popular with law enforcement agencies and private users. The 4506 has a magazine safety that prevents firing unless a magazine is in place, a firing pin lock to prevent discharge unless the trigger is pulled, and an ambidextrous manual safety on the rear of the frame. It is also designed to be simple and quick to strip for maintenance, and has a bevelled magazine well to assist rapid loading. Three-dot sights are fitted, for faster point-and-shoot acquisition, and recently manufactured third-generation Smith & Wesson semi-automatics have an accessory rail mounted in front of the trigger guard, under the barrel.

SPECIFICATIONS

COUNTRY OF ORIGIN:	*United States*
DATE:	*1988*
CALIBRE:	*11.43mm (0.45in)*
OPERATION:	*Double-action revolver*
WEIGHT:	*1.16kg (2lb 10oz)*
BARREL LENGTH:	*125mm (5in)*
MUZZLE VELOCITY:	*49m/s (160f/s)*
FEED:	*Eight-round box magazine*

SMITH & WESSON 4506 FACTS:

- .45 ACP calibre semi-automatic pistol
- Double-action with manual safety
- One of many variants on the same basic weapon

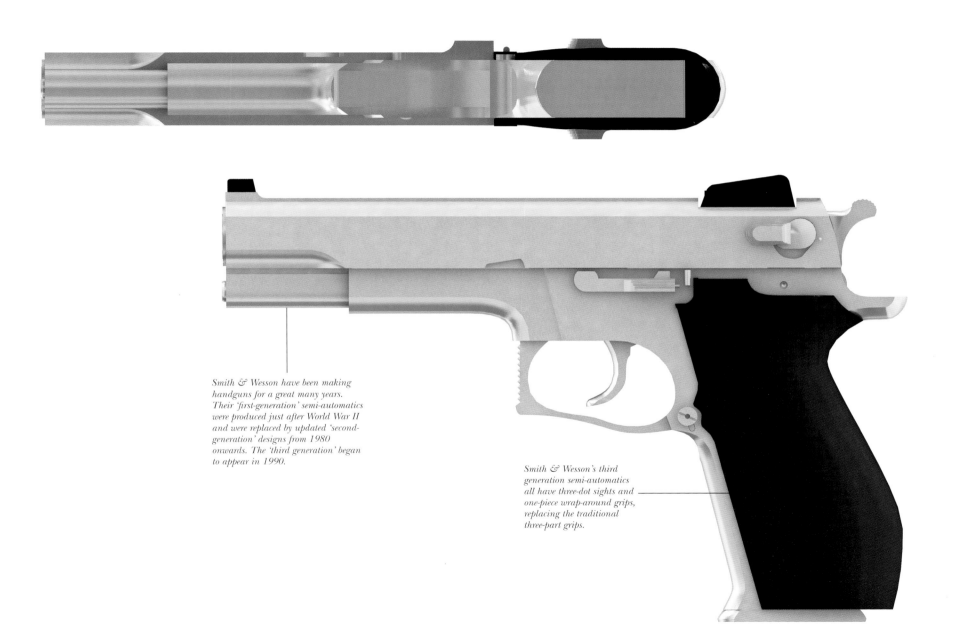

Smith & Wesson have been making handguns for a great many years. Their 'first-generation' semi-automatics were produced just after World War II and were replaced by updated 'second-generation' designs from 1980 onwards. The 'third generation' began to appear in 1990.

Smith & Wesson's third generation semi-automatics all have three-dot sights and one-piece wrap-around grips, replacing the traditional three-part grips.

BARRICADE POSITION

When firing over an obstruction or solid cover, many firearms experts advocate the 'barricade position', using the object as a rest for the weapon. A kneeling position is generally advised. However, some authorities suggest that it is better to be positioned some way back from a cover that has a flat top (such as a car), to reduce the possibility of an incoming round ricocheting upward from the flat surface and scoring a hit. It is also important to understand the difference between 'cover' and 'concealment'. Cover will stop a bullet; concealment merely makes a hit less likely. Most parts of a car offer concealment but little cover, though they may deflect a shot. Only the engine block can be considered as cover.

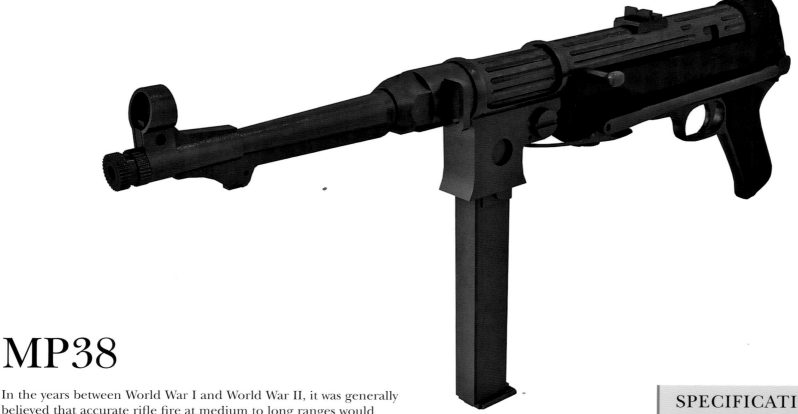

MP38

In the years between World War I and World War II, it was generally
believed that accurate rifle fire at medium to long ranges would
determine the outcome of infantry combat. Submachineguns, or machine pistols as they were generally
called at the time, were thus not seen as a significant infantry weapon. However, a need for light
automatic weaponry was perceived, to grant additional firepower to paratroops and vehicle
crewmembers. The German army thus funded the development of the MP36, a prototype weapon that
went into production in simplified form as the MP38, which in turn was developed into the MP40 via an
interim model designated MP38/40. The MP38 and its derivatives used a blowback mechanism and had
no selector switch, although single shots and short bursts were possible with careful trigger control.
These weapons were expensive to produce compared to the bolt-action rifles used by most infantry. They
remained the province of special units such as paratroops for most of the war, though the increasing
incidence of close-quarters urban combat led to wider issue of submachineguns in the later years. With its
relatively low rate of fire (500rpm) and 32-round magazine, the MP38 offered good firepower and, with
the stock folded, was short and handy for close-quarters fighting. However, a tendency to use the long
magazine as a foregrip could lead to stoppages. Pulling the magazine back moved it out of alignment and
could result in a failure to feed ammunition into the breech.

SPECIFICATIONS

COUNTRY OF ORIGIN:	Germany
DATE:	1936
CALIBRE:	9mm (0.35in) Parabellum
OPERATION:	Blowback
WEIGHT:	3.97kg (8lb 12oz)
OVERALL LENGTH:	Stock extended 832mm (32.75in); Stock folded 629mm (24.76in)
BARREL LENGTH:	248mm (9.76in)
MUZZLE VELOCITY:	380m/sec (1247ft/sec)
FEED:	32-round box magazine

MP38 FACTS:

● 9 x 19mm (0.35 x 0.75in) calibre submachinegun
● Fully automatic only
● Expensive to produce

The MP38 and its derivatives are often wrongly referred to as 'Schmeissers' after the designer of Germany's first submachinegun, the MP18.

MP38s were often issued to squad leaders, who were expected to spend more time directing their troops than firing at the enemy. The extra firepower afforded by an automatic weapon was useful in an emergency.

MP38

RISK OF BURNING

Although an effective weapon, the MP38 and its derivatives had flaws. The correct way to support the weapon was to grip either the magazine well or the underside of the weapon near it, but there was little to stop the user from burning his left hand on the hot barrel if his hand position was incorrect. This made gripping the magazine itself seem attractive, but this often led to stoppages. The long magazine made the weapon difficult to use from a prone position – not a huge problem, as submachineguns are intended for fast-moving combat in close terrain. The MP38 and MP40 were general issue only to paratroopers and some assault formations; most infantrymen were still equipped with rifles.

Thompson M1928

John T. Thompson invented the word 'submachinegun' to describe his delayed blowback-operated, fully automatic, pistol-calibre weapon, which first went into production as the M1921. The M1928 model featured slight improvements to the action, which reduced the rate of fire. This model was adopted by the US military. Chambered for the powerful .45 ACP round that was in use in US military sidearms, the Thompson offered excellent stopping power at fairly short ranges, and good firepower from its 20- or 30-round magazine. A 50-round drum magazine was also available. The Thompson won notoriety during the Prohibition era, but proved an excellent military weapon in the hands of paratroops and vehicle crews. Although heavy and expensive to manufacture, it was sufficiently effective to remain in use through World War II and the Vietnam era. Some police departments still had Thompsons in their armoury in the 1980s. A number of variants were produced. Some were fairly minor, such as M1928s with a pistol-style 'assault' foregrip, while others involved a certain amount of redesign. The M1 version was created to make mass-production simpler and cheaper. It could not take the 50-round drum magazine but was otherwise similar. Other versions never reached production, such as the M1923 'Military Model', which was chambered for the slightly heavier .45 Remington-Thompson round and had a longer barrel with a bayonet mount and provision for a bipod. This variant was intended to extend the effective range of the Thompson out to about 600m (1969ft), but in the end the more conventional M1928 proved more suitable.

SPECIFICATIONS

COUNTRY OF ORIGIN:	United States
DATE:	1938
CALIBRE:	11.43mm (0.45in) ACP
OPERATION:	Delayed blowback
WEIGHT:	4.88kg (10lb 12oz)
OVERALL LENGTH:	857mm (33.75in)
BARREL LENGTH:	266mm (10.5in)
MUZZLE VELOCITY:	920ft/sec (280m/sec)
FEED:	18-, 20- or 30-round detachable box magazine

THOMPSON M1928 FACTS:

- .45 ACP calibre submachinegun
- Excellent stopping power but fairly short effective range
- Heavy but robust and reliable

The M1928 was fitted with a Cutts Compensator, which countered muzzle climb due to recoil by venting some of the propellant gases upwards. This feature was not used on the M1 version.

The Thompson's 700rpm rate of fire was excellent for its originally envisaged role as a 'trench sweeper', and was found useful in counter-ambush situations. However, the .45 ACP round did not penetrate cover well.

URBAN WARFARE

The M1928 was effective at the same sort of range as the M1 carbines carried by this gunner's companions, and it had better stopping power. The .45 ACP round was an excellent manstopper, though a lack of penetration made it ineffective against hostiles who were under even light cover. Despite this, the Thompson was a good weapon for urban warfare, where buildings might have to be cleared with grenades and short-range combat. The high-capacity drum magazine seemed ideal for this role, but was abandoned due to two shortcomings: it was prone to stoppages, which could be fatal in a short-range firefight, and it was noisy, which could compromise a stealthy approach and allow the enemy to stage an ambush.

Sten Mk II

The Sten series of submachineguns were basic and rather crude, but they had the advantage of being cheap and simple to manufacture. This was exactly what Britain needed at a time when invasion seemed imminent. The Mk II Sten was perhaps the definitive model in the series. Constructed from cheap stamped-metal parts, these weapons could be (and were) thrown together using the most basic facilities. Some were made in school workshops. The Mk I and V Stens, created before and after the invasion threat respectively, were rather more sophisticated and refined, but the overall function was more or less the same. Stens could be prone to accidental discharge if knocked, and suffered from ammunition feed problems that were never rectified. Despite these drawbacks, the Sten was an effective weapon in close-quarters fighting, sufficiently so that it was copied by German manufacturers for the defence of Germany. It was also widely distributed to resistance fighters all over Europe. The Sten was capable of semi-automatic or full-automatic fire, by means of a cross-bolt passing through the trigger mechanism. This was pushed to the right for semi-automatic operation or to the left for full-automatic fire. In the latter mode the Sten was capable of 550 rounds per minute. A variant of the Mk II Sten, the Mk IIS or 'Silent Sten', was created by replacing the standard barrel with a barrel/silencer unit that could be fitted to any Mk II Sten. The weapon remained capable of full-automatic fire, though this was not recommended.

SPECIFICATIONS

COUNTRY OF ORIGIN:	United Kingdom
DATE:	1942
CALIBRE:	9mm (0.35in) Parabellum
OPERATION:	Blowback
WEIGHT:	2.95kg (6lb 8oz)
OVERALL LENGTH:	895mm (35.25in)
BARREL LENGTH:	196mm (7.71in)
MUZZLE VELOCITY:	380m/sec (1247ft/sec)
FEED:	32-round box magazine

STEN MK II FACTS:

- 9 x 19mm (0.35 x 0.75in) submachinegun
- Extremely cheap to manufacture
- Unreliable ammunition feed

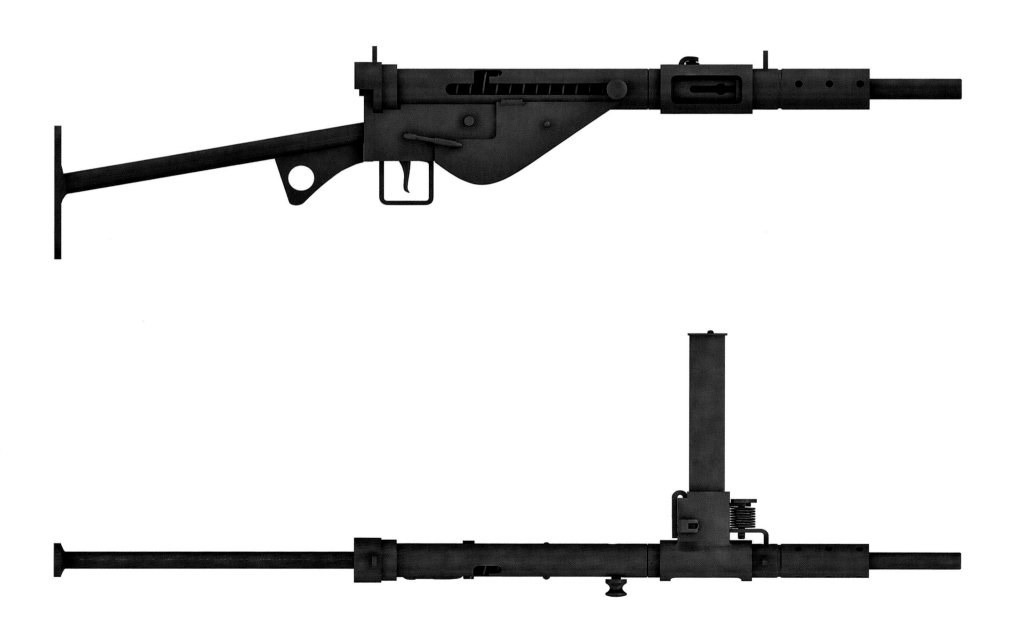

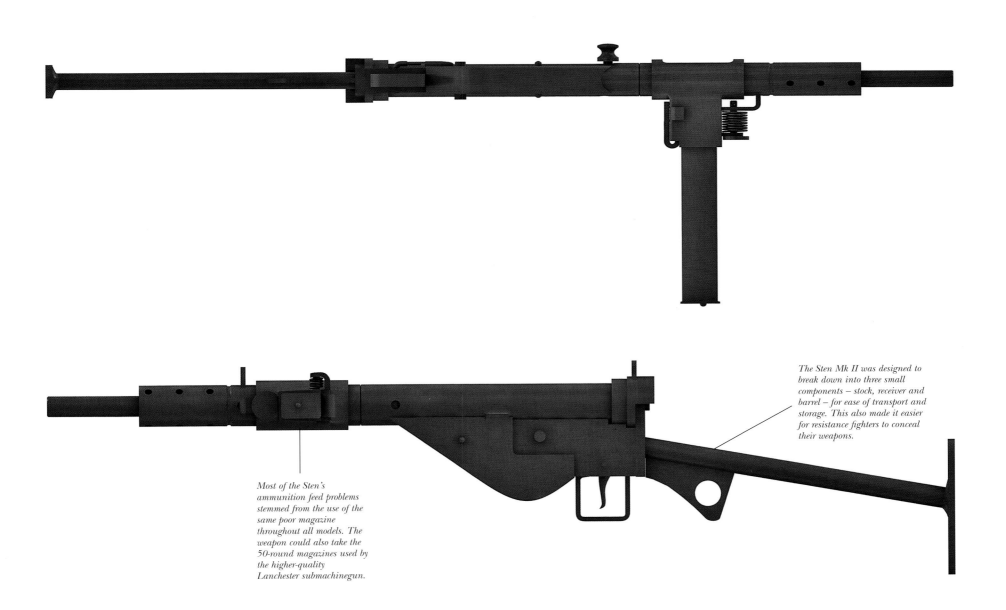

The Sten Mk II was designed to break down into three small components – stock, receiver and barrel – for ease of transport and storage. This also made it easier for resistance fighters to conceal their weapons.

Most of the Sten's ammunition feed problems stemmed from the use of the same poor magazine throughout all models. The weapon could also take the 50-round magazines used by the higher-quality Lanchester submachinegun.

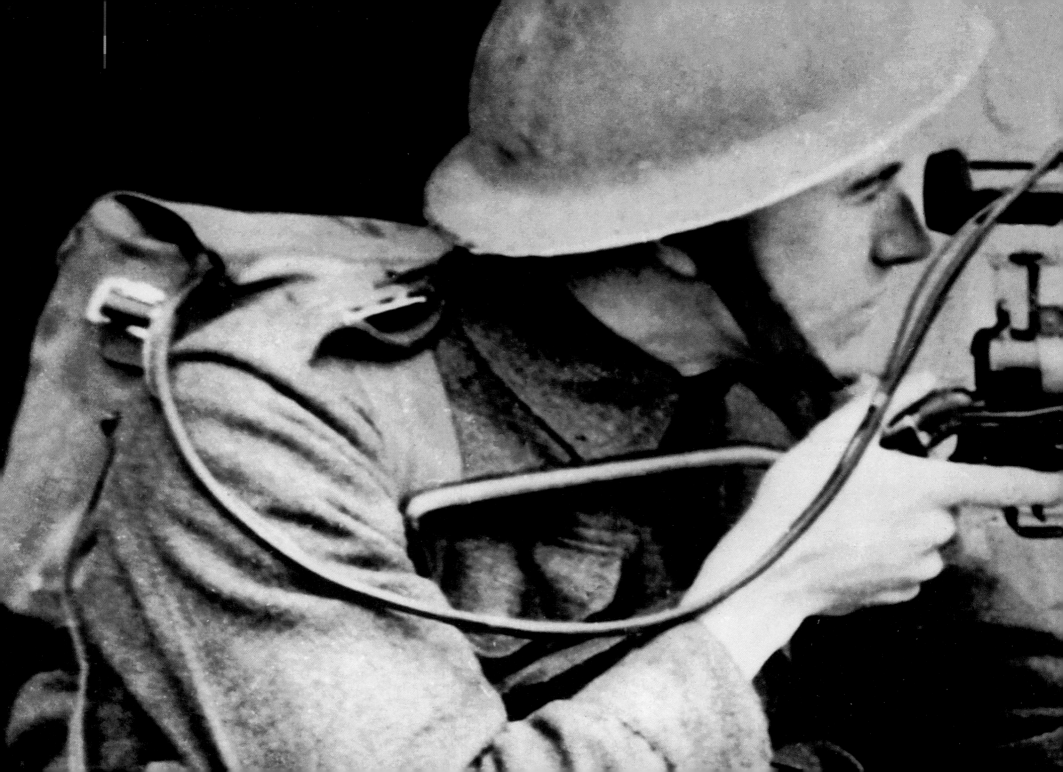

SILENT STEN

Although the Sten was a basic weapon, it was effective – and available in the huge numbers required. Stens were the basis for various experiments, including a successful silenced version and this rather crude infra-red sighted weapon for night fighting. Both the Allies and the Axis powers experimented with weapons that used an infra-red light and a detector during World War II. Similar devices were used on warships and tanks to illuminate their targets, probably a more effective use of this technology than mating it to a submachinegun whose main virtue was its lightness and easy handling. However, adding the lamp, battery pack and sight to the 'Silent Sten' did offer possibilities for special-operations personnel.

Uzi

The Uzi submachinegun is named after its inventor, Uziel Gal. Its design was revolutionary at the time but has been widely copied since. Rather than being constructed like a conventional rifle or carbine, with the magazine well in front of the trigger assembly, the Uzi uses a similar method to a semi-automatic pistol, with the magazine inserted through the handgrip. However, the method of operation is rather different to that of a handgun. The Uzi uses an internal bolt rather than an external slide, which reduces the weapon's cyclic rate to a manageable level. The Uzi fires from an open bolt – i.e. with the bolt locked in the rear position – which can affect accuracy and allow dust and dirt to enter the mechanism. However, it has proven reliable in combat. The standard Uzi submachinegun comes with a folding metal stock, though early models used a fixed wooden stock. It was issued to the Israeli military as a self-defence weapon for vehicle crews and support troops, and also to assault units. Although the Uzi has now been retired from Israeli military service, it remains in use elsewhere in the world. The standard Uzi was followed by the Mini-Uzi and Micro-Uzi, both of which are smaller versions of the standard weapon. Civilian versions, capable of semi-automatic fire only and designated '9mm carbines', are also offered on the open market. Most Uzis are chambered for 9mm (0.35in), but versions are available in other calibres.

SPECIFICATIONS

COUNTRY OF ORIGIN:	Israel
DATE:	1953
CALIBRE:	9mm (0.35in) Parabellum
OPERATION:	Blowback
WEIGHT:	3.7kg (8lb 2oz)
OVERALL LENGTH:	Stock extended 650mm (25.6in) Stock folded 470mm (18.5in)
BARREL LENGTH:	260mm (10.24in)
MUZZLE VELOCITY:	400m/sec (1312ft/sec)
FEED:	25- or 32-round box magazine

UZI FACTS:

- Compact 9 x 19mm (0.35 x 0.75in) submachinegun
- Smaller Mini-Uzi and Micro-Uzi variants also available
- Simple to strip and maintain

The Uzi is constructed
from cheap stamped metal
for the most part, which
reduces the cost of
manufacturing. Various
sizes of magazine are
available in addition to the
standard 32-round one.

The Uzi is fitted with a
fairly standard
safety/selector, which can
be set to safe, semi-
automatic or full-automatic
positions. There is also a
grip safety to prevent
discharge unless the
weapon is properly held.

CONFINED SPACES

Some military personnel require a weapon that offers good firepower but cannot carry a full-sized rifle or even a carbine due to the nature of their duties. The Uzi provided an ideal weapon for vehicle crews, combat engineers and similar troops who might have to defend themselves but whose primary role is not infantry combat. Not greatly larger than a handgun, an Uzi does not get in the way as much as a rifle or carbine, and is also highly suitable for close-quarters combat in the hands of assault troops. These characteristics have made it popular with law enforcement, security and hostage-rescue units, who may have to conceal their weapons or use them in very tight spaces.

MP5K

The Heckler & Koch MP5 has spawned a wide range of variants since it was introduced in 1966. These share the original weapon's excellent accuracy and reliability, making the MP5 a favourite with law enforcement agencies. All variants of the MP5 use H&K's roller-delayed blowback mechanism and share most characteristics, though the MP5K has a slightly higher cyclic rate than the standard version. The MP5K is a shortened variant intended primarily for covert use or VIP protection. It has a foregrip and no stock, and is optimized for close-range instinctive shooting. It is normally carried with a small (15-round) magazine but can take the standard MP5 30-round magazine if necessary. There are four main variants of the MP5K. The standard version has similar sights to a full-sized MP5, while the MP5KA1 has minimal sights and is as smooth as possible to facilitate a fast deployment from under clothing. The MP5KA5 is a version of the A1 with three-round burst capability. The corresponding burst-capable version of the standard MP5K is the MP5KA4. A new version of the MP5K was introduced in the 1990s, in the 'personal defence weapon' niche. Designated MP5K-PDW, this is essentially an MP5K fitted with a folding stock. The muzzle can take a silencer, and a laser pointer can also be fitted. The PDW variant is normally capable of semi-automatic or full-automatic fire, but can be adapted to add burst capability.

SPECIFICATIONS

COUNTRY OF ORIGIN:	Germany
DATE:	1972
CALIBRE:	9mm (0.35in) Parabellum
OPERATION:	Delayed blowback
WEIGHT:	2.1kg (4lb 10oz)
OVERALL LENGTH:	325mm (12.8in)
BARREL LENGTH:	115mm (4.53in)
MUZZLE VELOCITY:	375m/sec (1230ft/sec)
FEED:	15- or 30-round box magazine

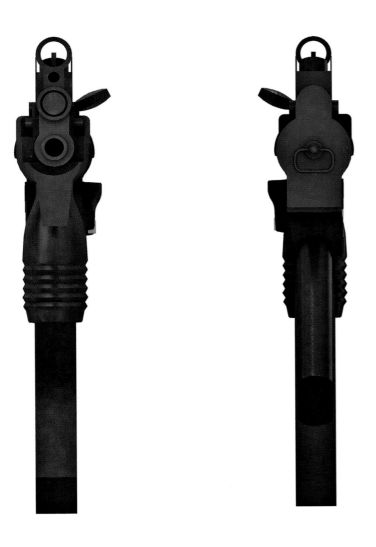

MP5K FACTS:

- 9 x 19mm (0.35 x 0.75in) submachinegun
- Extremely small dimensions
- Stockless, with a foregrip to assist controllability

Despite its small size, the MP5K
is very controllable under
autofire. The foregrip and pistol
grip are as widely spaced as
possible to give the user leverage
to counter muzzle climb.

The MP5 family use combined
safety/selector switch with modes
marked by one, three or many
bullets. Civilian models are
available, capable of semi-
automatic fire only.

LAW ENFORCEMENT

*The MP5 is popular with hostage-rescue and special law
enforcement units. It is accurate and controllable, yet
light and easy to handle in the confines of a building.
Just as importantly, the 9mm (0.35in) round used offers
good stopping power but will not penetrate walls or other
obstructions to any great extent. This is an important
consideration; law enforcement personnel cannot afford
collateral casualties. This makes rifle-calibre weapons
problematical, other than for snipers. A high-velocity
rifle bullet is a more effective man-stopper, but there is
the danger that it might pass through a wall and
injure an innocent. Conversely, a 9mm (0.35in)
submachinegun is more precise than a shotgun.*

Tec9 (TEC-DC9)

The family of weapons known colloquially by the designation DTEC-DC9 or Tec9 have their origins in a submachinegun intended for the military market. Derived from the venerable Carl Gustaf M45, this weapon was marketed by Interdynamic AB but failed to achieve market success. The firm Intratec was then set up to offer a semi-automatic version of the weapon to the US market. This was effectively a semi-automatic pistol fed from a large-capacity magazine located forward of the trigger assembly. The original TEC-DC9 could be converted to full-automatic operation with relative ease, though this is illegal in the United States and elsewhere. As a result, the weapon gained an unsavoury reputation, associated with criminal activity in much the same way that the Thompson SMG became associated with Prohibition-era gangsters. Later models were harder to convert. The weapon uses blowback operation and can be fed from a range of magazine sizes, starting at 10 rounds; 20-, 32- and 36-round magazines are not uncommon, with even larger capacities available. However, the 1996 Assault Weapons Ban in the United States specifically named this weapon as one of the banned models, largely because of its high capacity. As a result of the ban, a new version of the weapon, designated AB-10 but popularly still known as Tec9, was introduced. The AB-10 was supplied with 10-round magazines, but can accommodate the larger magazines of earlier versions.

SPECIFICATIONS

COUNTRY OF ORIGIN:	Sweden/United States
DATE:	1985
CALIBRE:	9mm (0.35in) Parabellum
OPERATION:	Blowback
WEIGHT:	1.23–1.4kg (2lb 11oz–3lb) depending on model
OVERALL LENGTH:	241–317mm (9.49–12.48in), depending on model
BARREL LENGTH:	76–127mm (2.99–5in) depending on model
MUZZLE VELOCITY:	764m/sec (2507ft/sec)
FEED:	10-, 20-, 32-, 36- and 50-round box magazine

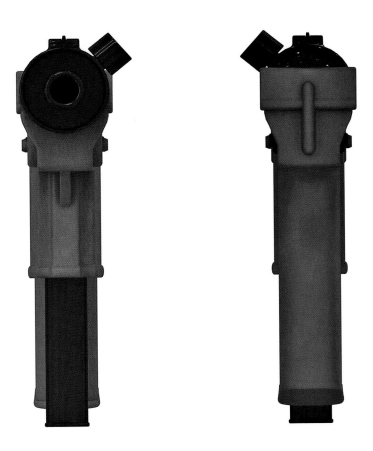

TEC9 (TEC-DC9) FACTS:

- 9 x 19mm (0.35 x 0.75in) semi-automatic pistol
- Derived from a submachinegun design
- Popularly associated with criminal activity

The original Tec9 fired from an open bolt and was easy to convert to full-automatic operation. Later models used a closed bolt and were much harder to convert.

The label Tec9 has been applied to several incarnations of the weapon, though most were marketed under slightly different names. All retained the submachinegun-like appearance of the original.

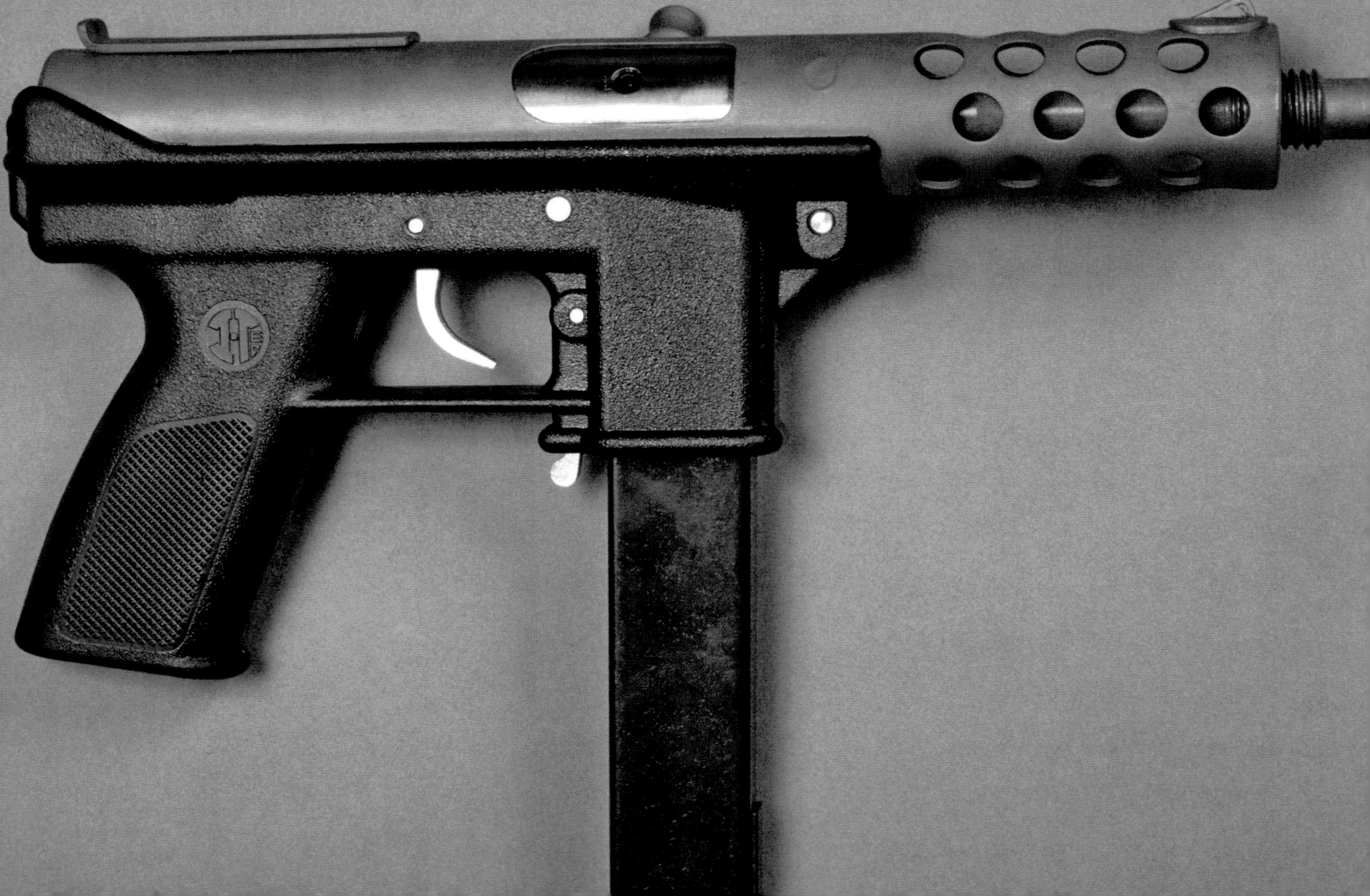

THE AFTER BAN

In 1994, the United States implemented a 10-year ban on 'semi-automatic assault weapons'. Different criteria were applied when defining a rifle, shotgun or handgun as an 'assault weapon'. In the case of the Tec9, it qualified as an assault weapon due to its possession of a ventilated barrel shroud and a high-capacity magazine located outside the handgrip. The AB10 (AB stands for 'After Ban') version did away with the barrel shroud and used a 10-round magazine, removing the features that defined it as an 'assault weapon' and thus making it legal to manufacture. The ban expired in 2004; there is no clear evidence as to whether it had any influence on criminal gun use.

Lee-Enfield

The Lee-Enfield rifle started its extremely long military career as a weapon that combined the magazine and action developed by J.P. Lee with a rifling system invented by W.E. Metford. Designated the Lee-Metford, this rifle was taken into British army service in 1888. An improved rifling system developed at the Enfield factory was adopted in 1895. The change was necessary to withstand the increased barrel temperatures generated by Cordite ammunition, which had replaced the black powder cartridges for which Metford rifling was developed. This version was designated Lee-Enfield Mk1. Experience in the Boer War, and a desire to save money by equipping both infantry and cavalry with the same weapon, led to an improved and shortened version designated Short Magazine Lee-Enfield, or SMLE. The SMLE was further developed during its service career, with a lighter and smaller 'Jungle Carbine' version appearing in the later years of World War II. Even after the Lee-Enfield was withdrawn from British Army service, versions remained in use as sniper rifles and for training purposes. The Lee-Enfield's 10-round internal magazine could be loaded from a charger, or a partially expended magazine could be topped up manually. It was also possible to fire and reload a single round, retaining a full magazine for emergency rapid fire. The bolt action was extremely smooth, allowing a designed rate of fire of 15 aimed rounds per minute. In practice, many personnel managed twice this or even more.

SPECIFICATIONS

COUNTRY OF ORIGIN:	*United Kingdom*
DATE:	*1907*
CALIBRE:	*7.69mm (0.303in)*
OPERATION:	*Bolt action*
WEIGHT:	*4kg (8lb 13oz)*
OVERALL LENGTH	*1130mm (44.5in)*
BARREL LENGTH	*635mm (25in)*
MUZZLE VELOCITY:	*744m/sec (2441ft/sec)*
FEED:	*10-round magazine, loaded with five-round charger clips*

LEE-ENFIELD FACTS:

- 7.69mm (0.303in) calibre bolt-action rifle
- High rate of fire possible for trained personnel
- 10-round internal magazine

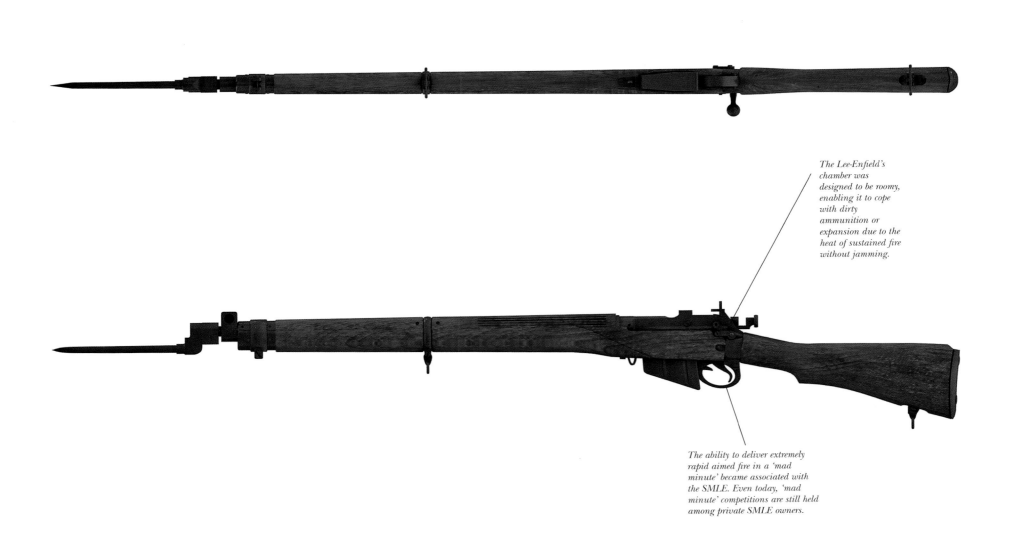

The Lee-Enfield's chamber was designed to be roomy, enabling it to cope with dirty ammunition or expansion due to the heat of sustained fire without jamming.

The ability to deliver extremely rapid aimed fire in a 'mad minute' became associated with the SMLE. Even today, 'mad minute' competitions are still held among private SMLE owners.

HIGHLY-EFFECTIVE

The Lee-Enfield rifle served, in various incarnations, through two world wars and beyond. It combined robust serviceability with accuracy and ease of use to create one of the finest military weapons of all time. Rifles of this type were developed in an era where long-range marksmanship was considered to be the key infantry skill. There are numerous reports of occasions during World War I when hostile troops thought they had encountered a machinegun position but were, in fact, up against a group of well-trained infantrymen with Lee-Enfields. Although more has perhaps been made of these tales than they may merit, the fact remains that the Lee-Enfield was a highly effective weapon in the right hands.

KAR-98

In 1898, Mauser produced a 7.92mm (0.31in) calibre bolt-action rifle fed from a five-round internal magazine. Designated Gewehr 98 (or G98), it was adopted into service with the German army. A shortened version, designated K-98 or KAR-98 (from the German word *Karabiner*, or carbine), was implemented soon afterward. The KAR-98 served though both world wars, and between the wars a version designated KAR-98k was introduced. This was a further shortened and lightened variant of the K98, and retained most of its characteristics. All versions of the weapon were built around Mauser's excellent bolt design, which used an extremely positive chambering and extraction system. The KAR-98 was normally loaded with a five-round stripper clip. Guides on the receiver assisted alignment, with the clip ejected once loading was complete. It could also be loaded manually, by feeding rounds one at a time into the breech. This method could be used to top up a partially-expended magazine or to fully load a weapon if pre-prepared clips were not available. The KAR-98 proved to be extremely robust and reliable. It could be easily maintained in the field and was accurate out to 600m (1969ft) using the integral iron sights. Few soldiers can shoot accurately at such a range, so 600m (1969ft) was more than adequate for combat in the open. For close combat a bayonet could be fitted, and during World War II a cup-type grenade launcher became available.

SPECIFICATIONS

COUNTRY OF ORIGIN:	Germany
DATE:	1935
CALIBRE:	7.92 x 57mm (0.31 x 2.24in) Mauser M98
OPERATION:	Bolt action
WEIGHT:	3.9kg (8lb 9oz)
OVERALL LENGTH	1107mm (43.58in)
BARREL LENGTH	600mm (23.62in)
MUZZLE VELOCITY:	755m/sec (2477ft/sec)
FEED:	Five-round box magazine

KAR-98 FACTS:

- 7.92 x 57mm (0.31 x 2.24in) calibre bolt-action rifle
- Five-round internal magazine
- Accurate and reliable

A 'sniper' version of the KAR-98 was created by adding a telescopic sight to an otherwise fairly ordinary example of the weapon. Slight variations in the manufacturing process produced weapons that were more or less accurate than the average; the best were selected for use by snipers.

The three-position safety catch allowed the rifle to be made safe with the bolt locked, safe with the bolt locked for loading, or ready to fire. It was designed to be easy to use with the thumb of the firing hand.

LONG-RANGE FIRE

The KAR-98 was designed to be used for long-range fire. Although subsequent versions were shorter, the rifle retained its inherent accuracy, which made it eminently suitable for use as a sniper weapon. No special modifications were needed, other than the fitting of a telescopic sight; weapons for snipers were selected from among those made by the normal process. The impact of snipers on any battle could be considerable; a single sniper could hold up an advance for some time until he was eliminated or driven off. Alternatively, snipers could eliminate officers and tank commanders to disrupt enemy forces. It was not uncommon for sniper teams to either slip through the enemy front line or stay behind as their comrades retreated. Either option allowed them to attack from an unexpected direction.

Winchester M70

The Winchester Model 70 was derived from an earlier Winchester rifle, the Model 54, which was in production until 1936. The new weapon incorporated a number of improvements, including a better trigger pull. It proved immensely popular with shooters and remains highly regarded today, especially as a deer rifle. In 1964, a number of changes were made to the Model 70. These were mainly for economic reasons, to allow the rifle to compete in a tough marketplace. The post-'64 Model 70 was never as popular as the pre-'64 version, but continued to sell well nevertheless. A number of versions of the M70 are in production today. Some incorporate modern techniques and technology, whilst others are 'classic' models using features of the pre-'64 rifle. Variants include a short-barrel model designed to be easy to carry in a police car, as well as a large number of civilian models intended for hunting or target shooting. The M70 has seen service as a military sniper rifle and with law enforcement agencies. It was issued during the Korean conflict and, in larger numbers, the Vietnam War. There, its most prominent user was the legendary Marine Corps sniper Carlos Hathcock. The M70 is available in a wide range of calibres. It is fed from an internal magazine whose capacity is determined by the ammunition used. Normally, five rounds are carried, plus one in the breech. Larger calibres such as .30–06 limit magazine capacity to four rounds, or three for magnum rounds such as .458 Winchester Magnum.

SPECIFICATIONS

COUNTRY OF ORIGIN:	United States
DATE:	1936
CALIBRE:	Various
OPERATION:	Bolt action
WEIGHT:	2.7–3.6kg (6–8lb)
OVERALL LENGTH:	1003–1187mm (39.5–46.75in) depending on model
BARREL LENGTH:	508, 559, 610 or 660mm (20, 22, 24 or 26in), depending on model
MUZZLE VELOCITY:	Various
FEED:	Three-round capacity (Magnum calibres); Four-round capacity (large calibres) Five-round capacity (standard calibres)

WINCHESTER M70 FACTS:

- Bolt-action rifle available in many calibres
- Accurate and reliable
- In production since 1936

The Model 70 was the standard US Marine Corps sniping rifle until the mid-1960s, when it was replaced by the Remington 700, which is designated M40 once modified for US military service.

The Model 70 is available in a number of variants, including a compact model intended for smaller shooters, lightweight and small-game models. At the other end of the scale, the Safari Express model is designed to hunt large game with heavy Magnum calibre rounds.

SNIPERS IN VIETNAM

Despite the experiences of World War II, in which snipers proved exceedingly effective, many nations neglected to maintain a strong sniping tradition in the years that followed. Conflict in that era proved sniping to be as important as ever, and sniper schools were re-established or expanded in armed forces worldwide. During the Vietnam War, snipers had an effect on enemy forces out of all proportion to their numbers. Snipers took a steady toll on enemy personnel, in some cases ambushing patrols using silenced rifles; the legendary Carlos Hathcock famously eliminated a North Vietnamese general. It was during this time that the sniper's role was expanded to include reconnaissance and, sometimes, forward observation for artillery or air support.

Martini-Henry

The Martini-Henry rifle was the result of combining a seven-groove rifling system invented by Alexander Henry and the falling-block breech mechanism devised by Frederich Martini. The resulting weapon was simple, robust, easy to maintain and accurate. It was adopted for service with the British army in 1871 and served until the end of the 1880s, when it was replaced by the Lee-Metford. Breech-loading rifles represented a significant increase in infantry firepower, giving troops a massive advantage over opponents equipped with weapons of previous generations. Britain was at the time engaged in a great deal of colonial warfare, pitting small but well-equipped and disciplined forces against large numbers of opponents far from support, so this capability was vital to the defence of the Empire. Sighted out to 1372m (4500ft), the Martini-Henry possessed good stopping power and was capable of rapid fire at need. A lever behind the trigger assembly opened the breech and ejected the spent round, then closed the breech around a manually-inserted round. The usual load was a 480-grain soft lead bullet, though a lighter round was available. Intended for use with the Martini-Henry carbine, this lighter round possessed a lesser range, accuracy and stopping power but was better than nothing for a force running short of ammunition. The ammunition used with the Martini-Henry was not flawless. A hot rifle could cause the thin-cased Boxer cartridge to cook off in the breech. This, and a tendency for ammunition to become mangled in transit, was rectified by the introduction of more robust (but heavier) cartridge cases.

SPECIFICATIONS

COUNTRY OF ORIGIN:	*United Kingdom*
DATE:	*1871*
CALIBRE:	*11.43mm (0.45in)*
OPERATION:	*Falling block breech-loader*
WEIGHT:	*3.9kg (8lb 9oz)*
OVERALL LENGTH:	*1129mm (48in)*
BARREL LENGTH:	*851mm (33.5in)*
MUZZLE VELOCITY:	*411m/sec (1350ft/sec)*
FEED:	*Single round, manual*

MARTINI-HENRY FACTS:

- .450 calibre lever-action breech-loading rifle
- Long range and good stopping power
- Reliable and easy to maintain

The Martini-Henry's recoil was not excessive, but the barrel did become hot very quickly. Many users wrapped cloth or leather around the barrel to protect their hands.

Depressing the lever drops the breechblock (hence the 'falling-block' designation) and cocks the weapon whilst extracting the spent round. A round is manually placed in the breech and the weapon brought to firing condition by returning the level to its initial position.

NAVAL INFANTRY

The naval landing party was an essential part of British colonial power-projection. Put ashore from an armoured cruiser to deal with whatever trouble surfaced, such parties were composed of sailors, not soldiers. Their infantry training was of necessity highly abbreviated, but naval personnel were nevertheless trained to carry out basic infantry evolutions. These included skirmishing, volley fire and the formation of a square to repel cavalry or the charge of native warriors armed with hand weapons. The Martini-Henry rifle was carried in large numbers aboard ships patrolling the colonial stations, and saw action in all corners of the world. Naval infantry also took part in large-scale campaigns, usually to make up numbers because there were never enough troops available. Sailors sometimes campaigned ashore for extended periods.

MP44/StG44

Experience in the early years of World War II demonstrated that modern combat was likely to take place at relatively short ranges, often in urban terrain, and that concentrated firepower was at least as desirable as long-range accuracy in a service rifle. One solution might have been to issue submachineguns more widely, but this would create a situation where a proportion of infantry would be powerless at ranges over 100m (328ft). A single weapon, capable of accurate fire at a reasonable range yet handy enough to be effective in close-quarters urban fighting, was desirable. The result was the weapon originally designated MP (machine-pistol)-44 but quickly renamed a 'storm rifle' – i.e. what would become known as an assault rifle. The Sturmgewehr-44 offered an effective compromise. Fed from a 30-round magazine and firing at 500rpm, it had the firepower of a submachinegun but was effective out to 400m (1312ft) or more. The StG44 used a short cartridge with reduced range, power and accuracy over the battle rifles of the period, but this was offset by volume of fire and reduced recoil. Lighter cartridges also allowed personnel to carry more ammunition, which was necessary given the high rate of expenditure when using automatic fire. The StG44 was sufficiently successful that it was copied or used as the basis of other weapons in many nations, and proved the concept of the lightweight, automatic assault rifle that is still in use today.

SPECIFICATIONS

COUNTRY OF ORIGIN:	Germany
DATE:	1943
CALIBRE:	7.92 x 33mm (0.31 x 1.29in) Kurz
OPERATION:	Gas-operated, tilting bolt
WEIGHT:	5.22kg (11lb 8oz)
OVERALL LENGTH	940mm (37in)
BARREL LENGTH	419mm (16.5in)
MUZZLE VELOCITY:	685m/sec (2247ft/sec)
FEED:	30-round detachable box magazine

MP44/StG44 FACTS:

- 7.92 x 33mm (0.31 x 1.29in) calibre assault rifle
- First of the type anywhere in the world
- Capable of semi-automatic or fully-automatic fire

The StG44 receiver was constructed of stamped steel, creating a relatively heavy weapon that was also expensive to produce. Heavy construction may have been a factor in the weapon's impressive resistance to horrific weather conditions on the Eastern Front.

The StG44's selector is a push-button device located just behind the safety catch. Troops were trained to use semi-automatic fire as much as possible, switching to full-automatic in emergencies such as close combat with submachinegun-armed opponents.

RIFLEMAN'S WEAPON

Although the StG44 was designed, to a great extent, to counter Soviet submachineguns, it was entirely effective as a traditional rifleman's weapon. It was effective out to about 400m (1312ft), which is further than most soldiers can shoot accurately. At such distances harassing fire, perhaps using bursts of full-automatic, is as likely to be effective as deliberate marksmanship for the average soldier. Of course, this used up large amounts of ammunition, so German troops armed with the StG44 were encouraged to take single aimed shots except in an emergency. However, the concept of using assault rifles for harassing or suppressive fire became commonplace in the years after World War II, resulting in a prodigious ammunition expenditure in return for a low number of enemy casualties.

AK47

Kalashnikov's AK47 is arguably the most successful assault rifle design of all time; certainly it was widely copied and spawned a host of variants. Chambered for 7.62 x 39mm (0.3 x 1.54in) ammunition, it is notable for its ability to keep on working, no matter what torments are inflicted upon it. It is highly tolerant of dirt and general mistreatment, and can be operated while wearing heavy gloves. The AK47 was designed to equip a mass army composed of conscripts with relatively little training. It is intended primarily for engagements at ranges out to about 250m (820ft), and beyond this distance is significantly inaccurate. However, most soldiers cannot shoot accurately at long range, and the AK47 is entirely adequate for long-range suppressive or harassing fire. An upgraded version, designated AKM, appeared in 1959. Among other improvements, the AKM has a muzzle brake to reduce muzzle climb. Recoil is still significant, however, making automatic fire difficult to control. A number of other weapons have been derived from the AK47, including the Finnish Valmet and the Israeli Galil. These are often built to a higher quality standard than the original weapon, but retain many of its features. The AKM, along with earlier AK47s, have been widely supplied worldwide in addition to arming the forces of the former Warsaw Pact. Vast numbers have also found their way onto the black market and have become associated with insurgent groups and militias in troubled regions.

SPECIFICATIONS

COUNTRY OF ORIGIN:	Russia
DATE:	1947
CALIBRE:	7.62 x 39mm (0.3 x 1.54in) M1943
OPERATION:	Gas
WEIGHT:	5.13kg (11lb 5oz)
OVERALL LENGTH:	869mm (34.21in)
BARREL LENGTH:	414mm (16.3in)
MUZZLE VELOCITY:	710m/sec (2330ft/sec)
FEED:	30-round box magazine

AK47 FACTS:

- 7.62 x 39mm (0.3 x 1.54in) calibre assault rifle
- Extremely common worldwide with many variants
- Extremely rugged and reliable

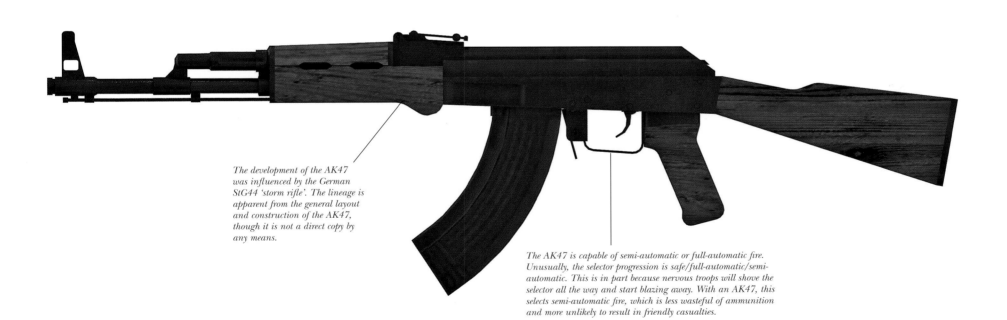

The development of the AK47 was influenced by the German StG44 'storm rifle'. The lineage is apparent from the general layout and construction of the AK47, though it is not a direct copy by any means.

The AK47 is capable of semi-automatic or full-automatic fire. Unusually, the selector progression is safe/full-automatic/semi-automatic. This is in part because nervous troops will shove the selector all the way and start blazing away. With an AK47, this selects semi-automatic fire, which is less wasteful of ammunition and more unlikely to result in friendly casualties.

LOW MAINTENANCE

The AK47 and its derivatives are popular with military forces and law enforcement agencies worldwide, not least because they require little care to remain functional. This is important when equipping a conscript or militia force whose personnel cannot be relied upon to properly look after their equipment. The reliability and good stopping power of the AK series are valued by police forces in very troubled areas of the world, where officers may be required to deal with heavily armed gangs far from any backup. Some AK rifles are fitted with a fixed wooden stock, but a folding metal one is generally a better choice for law enforcement personnel, who may have to move in and out of buildings or vehicles in the course of their duties.

M16A1/A2 + M203

In the years after the end of the Korean conflict, the US military concluded that its future needs would be best met by a lightweight rifle capable of automatic fire, using a smaller cartridge than the 7.62mm (0.3in) round then in front-line use. The M16 was introduced during the Vietnam War, and ran into teething troubles straightaway. It had been designed to need minimal maintenance, but the jungle conditions in Southeast Asia proved too much for it. A series of improvements created an effective rifle in the M16A1 and M16A2 models. The A2 version was designed to be more robust and had different rifling. More noticeably, it was not a fully automatic weapon but instead could use semi-automatic or three-round burst modes. The theory behind this was sound; burst fire offered the capability for high-volume fire without wasting as much ammunition as a long automatic burst. However, the M16A2 suffered from a number of problems surrounding the burst mechanism: the cam system used to control burst causes trigger pull to vary considerably, adversely affecting accuracy. The M16 rifle is often used with the M203 40mm (1.57in) grenade launcher. Mounted under the barrel of the rifle, the M203 allows an infantry soldier to deliver high explosive, smoke or other grenades out to several hundred metres. By using the M16's stock and fittings for support, the M203 permits a soldier to function as a grenadier without depriving the squad of one of its riflemen.

SPECIFICATIONS

COUNTRY OF ORIGIN:	United States
DATE:	1960
CALIBRE:	5.56mm (0.22in) M193
OPERATION:	Gas
WEIGHT:	2.86kg (6lb 5oz)
OVERALL LENGTH:	990mm (39in)
BARREL LENGTH:	508mm (20in)
MUZZLE VELOCITY:	1000m/sec (3280ft/sec)
FEED:	30-round detachable box magazine

M16A1/A2 + M203 FACTS:

- 5.56 x 45mm (0.22 x 1.7in) calibre assault rifle
- Versions in service since 1963
- Under-barrel grenade launcher can be fitted

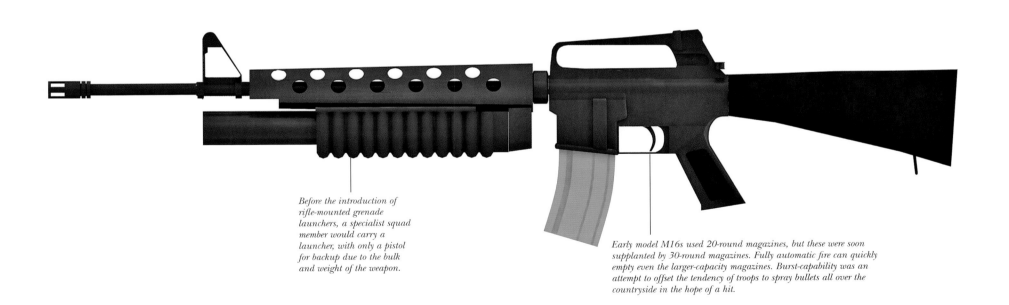

Before the introduction of rifle-mounted grenade launchers, a specialist squad member would carry a launcher, with only a pistol for backup due to the bulk and weight of the weapon.

Early model M16s used 20-round magazines, but these were soon supplanted by 30-round magazines. Fully automatic fire can quickly empty even the larger-capacity magazines. Burst-capability was an attempt to offset the tendency of troops to spray bullets all over the countryside in the hope of a hit.

MORE AMMUNITION

The M16 will forever be associated with the Vietnam War, though it was only the primary US infantry weapon for a part of the conflict. The main advantage offered by the lighter 5.56mm (0.22in) round used by the M16 was the ability to carry more ammunition than previously. High-volume fire was often the only way to hit fleeting targets in the jungle, requiring a generous supply of spare magazines. Hit rates were very low during the Vietnam conflict, partly due to this factor and partly since troops who have plenty of ammunition and a fast-firing weapon are liable to hose it around the countryside when under stress. The burst-capable M16A2 was developed in part to offset this tendency, requiring repeated trigger pulls to fire off a whole magazine.

Dragunov

Developed in the early 1960s for the Soviet armed forces, the Dragunov SVD is a highly accurate semi-automatic rifle. It uses a short-stroke piston to operate the bolt. This minimizes internal shifting of weight during a shot, which could reduce accuracy. The Dragunov is chambered for 7.62 x 54mm (0.29 x 2.13in) ammunition. Although of the same diameter as the ammunition used in the AK47, the Dragunov's cartridges are longer and contain more propellant, resulting in a far higher muzzle velocity and consequently greater range and accuracy. Sniper-grade ammunition is normally issued, though ordinary rounds can be used along with specialist ammunition such as armour-piercing rounds. This rifle was not intended specifically for snipers in the usual sense, but instead was meant to be carried by a soldier within an infantry squad. This marksman would be able to engage targets beyond the usual ranges managed by combat troops, out to about 600m (1969ft). The rifle does make an excellent sniping weapon, however, and has seen considerable service in this role. Variants include the SVD-S, which has a plastic pistol grip and a folding metal stock. This is designed to lock very firmly in place, ensuring a stable rest for the weapon. A civilian hunting version is marketed under the designation Tigr (or Tiger), and the weapon has been widely copied in other countries. Some copies are cosmetic only, in that they have different internal workings, but direct copies are made in Iraq and China, among other users.

SPECIFICATIONS

COUNTRY OF ORIGIN:	Russia
DATE:	1963
CALIBRE:	7.62mm (0.29in)
OPERATION:	Gas
WEIGHT:	4.31kg (9lb 8oz)
OVERALL LENGTH:	1225mm (48.2in)
BARREL LENGTH:	610mm (24in)
MUZZLE VELOCITY:	828m/ecs (2720ft/sec)
FEED:	10-round detachable

DRAGUNOV FACTS:

- 7.62 x 54mm (0.29 x 2.13in) semi-automatic sniper rifle
- Accurate to 1200m (3937ft) with iron sights alone
- Can mount a standard AK assault rifle bayonet

The Dragunov SVD comes with a good set of iron sights, but is usually paired with a 4X optical telescopic sight. It can take a range of other accessories, including infra-red and high-magnification sights.

During the Soviet era, doctrine required an SVD-armed marksman to be included in every infantry platoon. This soldier was tasked with engaging high-value targets such as officers and support gunners whilst his squad mates carried out more general combat tasks.

REMOTE AREAS

Evaluation of rifles captured in Afghanistan showed them to be very effective, especially in the long-range engagements that are common in remote areas. Larger-calibre weapons such as the Dragunov are arguably superior to the small-calibre assault rifles that arm most modern infantry in this situation, generating new interest in more powerful infantry rifles. The Soviet doctrine for which the SVD was developed was paralleled in the West with the use of Designated Marksmen – soldiers who are equipped with an accurate long-range rifle and trained to a high standard of marksmanship but who are not full snipers. Designated Marksmen provide extra capabilities to an infantry formation rather than operating as a separate asset.

M82/M107 Barrett

The origins of the M82 'Light Fifty' sniping rifle probably lie in the use during the Vietnam War of .50 calibre machineguns jury-rigged with telescopic sights for long-range sniping. In the 1980s, the Barrett Firearms Company began experimenting with a large-calibre rifle, which matured into the M82 family. The M82A1 was bought in numbers by the Swedish army, and soon afterwards by the US military. It saw action in the Gulf War as an anti-materiel rifle and for explosive ordnance disposal. It has also been used in the anti-personnel role, of course, but this is not its primary mode of operation. It is primarily a means of attacking valuable but relatively fragile equipment, such as radar units, light vehicles and communications equipment. The M82A2 version was essentially the same rifle reconfigured in a 'bullpup' layout, with the magazine well and feed mechanism behind the trigger assembly to reduce the overall length of the weapon. It was not a success, however, and did not go into large-scale production. Other variants include an experimental 25mm (0.98in) grenade launcher. Whilst effective, this weapon produced too much recoil to be useable. The current Barrett rifle in US military service is designated M107. This is a slightly modified version of the M82A1, with a longer accessory rail and other fairly minor changes. A lighter version is under development, along with a shorter variant for use inside vehicles and helicopters.

SPECIFICATIONS

COUNTRY OF ORIGIN:	United States
DATE:	1982
CALIBRE:	12.7mm (0.50in
OPERATION:	Short-recoil, semi-automatic
WEIGHT:	14.7kg (32lb 6oz)
OVERALL LENGTH:	1549mm (60.98in)
BARREL LENGTH:	838mm (33in)
MUZZLE VELOCITY:	843m/sec (2800ft/sec)
FEED:	11-round box magazine

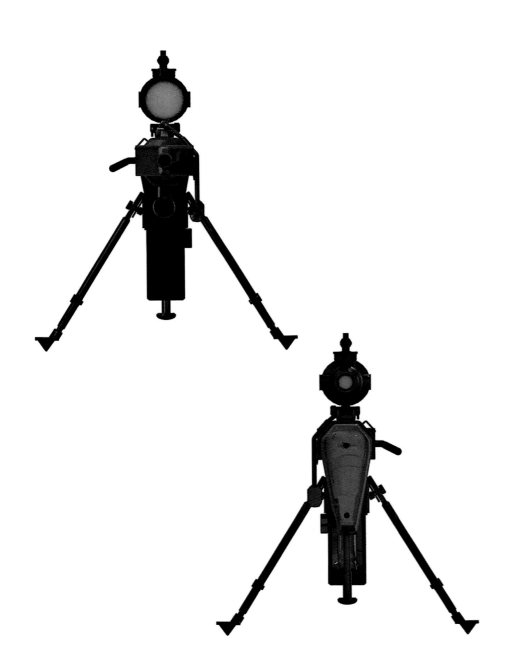

M82/M107 BARRETT FACTS:

- .50 calibre semi-automatic anti-materiel rifle
- Effective range 1800m (5906ft) or more
- Capable of firing special (e.g. explosive) ammunition

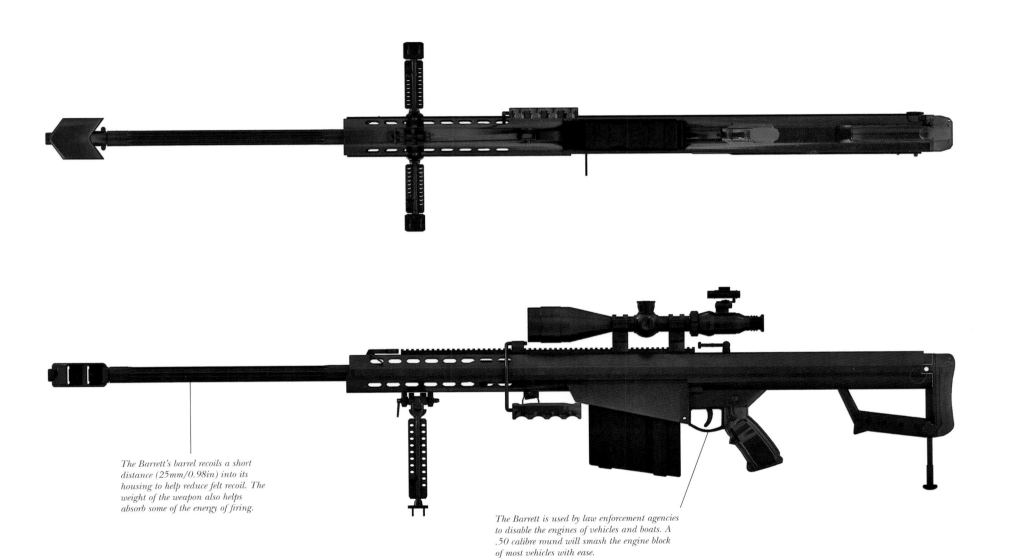

The Barrett's barrel recoils a short distance (25mm/0.98in) into its housing to help reduce felt recoil. The weight of the weapon also helps absorb some of the energy of firing.

The Barrett is used by law enforcement agencies to disable the engines of vehicles and boats. A .50 calibre round will smash the engine block of most vehicles with ease.

EXTREME LONG-RANGE

Heavy anti-materiel rifles represent the largest a rifle-type weapon can be whilst remaining man-portable. They are capable of hitting a human-sized target at very great ranges, which can be useful under a variety of circumstances. The elimination of key personnel is, of course, useful, but extreme long-range sniping can also be used in regions such as Afghanistan, where it may be necessary to remove hostiles from a vantage point on the other side of a deep valley. The ability to deny the enemy reconnaissance data, or to destroy their communications equipment to prevent a report being made, may justify the effort and expense of deploying this weapon along with a sniper who has the skill to make use of it.

M4A1

Developed from the M16A2, the M4 can be considered a carbine form of the M16 rifle. Mechanical parts are interchangeable and the M4 uses the same ammunition, magazines and accessories such as the M203 grenade launcher. However, it is significantly smaller and lighter due to its shorter barrel and redesigned stock. The move towards carbine-type weapons was a logical progression given the nature of modern warfare. A shorter weapon is useful when moving in and out of vehicles, and in close-quarters urban combat. This comes at the price of a reduction in long-range accuracy and a slight reduction in muzzle velocity due to the shorter barrel, but the short range of most modern combat renders this drawback negligible in effect most of the time. Another advantage of using a carbine is that all troops can be issued the same weapon. Rear-area units, logistics formations and similar troops who are not expected to have to engage in direct infantry combat are usually issued a smaller, lighter weapon that will not interfere in their tasks as much as a full-sized rifle. Commonality of weapons across all types of unit simplifies logistics, maintenance and training. The M4 carbine is standard-issue for US Army troops and Air Force security personnel. The US Marine Corps issues it instead of a handgun to personnel who would normally only carry a sidearm, such as offices and medics.

SPECIFICATIONS

COUNTRY OF ORIGIN:	United States
DATE:	1994
CALIBRE:	5.56mm (0.22in) NATO
OPERATION:	Gas
WEIGHT:	3.99kg (8lb 13oz)
OVERALL LENGTH:	1006mm (39.63in)
BARREL LENGTH:	508mm (20in)
MUZZLE VELOCITY:	853m/sec (2800ft/sec)
FEED:	20- or 30-round detachable box magazine

M4A1 FACTS:

- 5.56 x 45mm (0.22 x 1.77in) calibre fully-automatic carbine
- Parts compatible with M16 family of rifles
- Light and handy

The M4 has a Picatinny rail along the top of the receiver. This is often used to attach the carrying handle, but can mount a range of sights and other accessories.

The M4 uses a telescoping stock rather than the more usual solid stock. This is not only lighter but also allows the weapon to be quickly adjusted to suit a different firer.

PICATINNY RAILS

Modern firearms users often want to add a range of accessories to their weapons to enhance capabilities under various circumstances. There is a considerable difference of opinion about which sighting aid or other device is the most useful. Thus many weapons now carry one or more Picatinny rails (named for the Picatinny armoury), which are standard fittings that enable all manner of devices to be fixed. This M4 has been fitted with a vertical foregrip and tactical flashlight on the under-barrel rail and a red dot sight on the sight rail. Any accessory compatible with the standard Picatinny rail can be quickly added to the weapon without any need for modifications; for example, the red dot sight can be easily swapped for a telescopic sight.

Lewis Gun

The Lewis machine gun was developed from an earlier and much more complex weapon by Isaac Newton Lewis, who struggled to sell it to the US military from 1911 to 1913. He then offered it to European armies, with Belgium and then Britain adopting the weapon. The Lewis gun was deployed in vast numbers by British forces, with numbers rising from four per battalion in 1915 to 46 per battalion in 1917. The US military eventually adopted the weapon, though it was supplanted by the Browning Automatic Rifle. Versions used by the navy and aboard vehicles were much the same as the infantry model, but for aircraft use a lightened variant was developed. High-speed airflow over the weapon cooled it sufficiently well that the large cooling jacket could be removed without much danger of the gun overheating during sustained fire. Fed from a top-mounted ammunition drum holding 47 rounds, the Lewis was accurate out to about 600m (1969ft). Rate of fire could be regulated by adjusting a spring; 500–600rpm was commonest. A larger 97-round drum was developed for airborne use, not least due to the difficulty of reloading while flying an aircraft. Although somewhat expensive to produce, the Lewis gun was reliable and effective, and light enough to be integrated into infantry squads. This permitted attacking forces to bring their machinegun support forward with them, something that was not possible with the tripod-mounted medium machineguns of the day.

SPECIFICATIONS

COUNTRY OF ORIGIN:	United States
DATE:	1914
CALIBRE:	7.69mm (0.303in)
OPERATION:	Gas, air-cooled
WEIGHT:	11.8kg (26lb)
OVERALL LENGTH:	1280mm (50.5in)
BARREL LENGTH:	965mm (38in)
MUZZLE VELOCITY:	745m/s (2444ft/s)
FEED:	47-round drum magazine

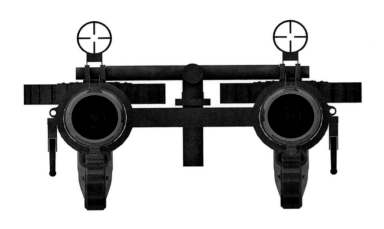

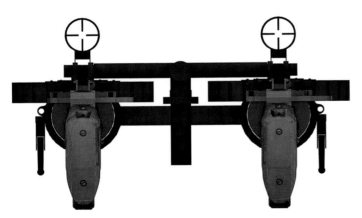

LEWIS GUN FACTS:

- .303 calibre light machinegun
- Top-mounted 47-round drum magazine
- Light enough to serve in the squad support role

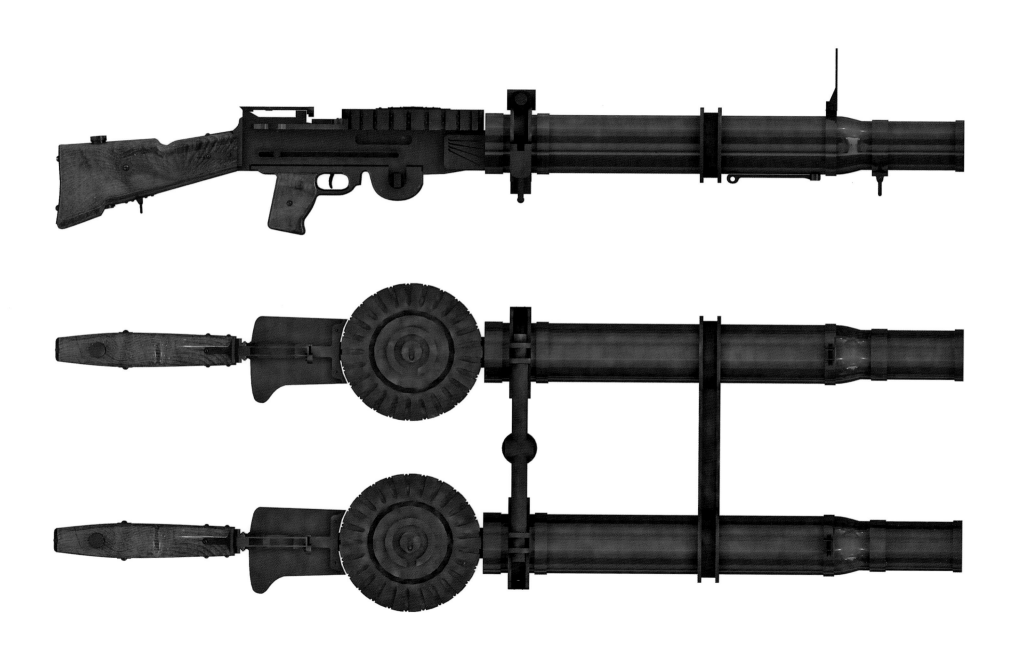

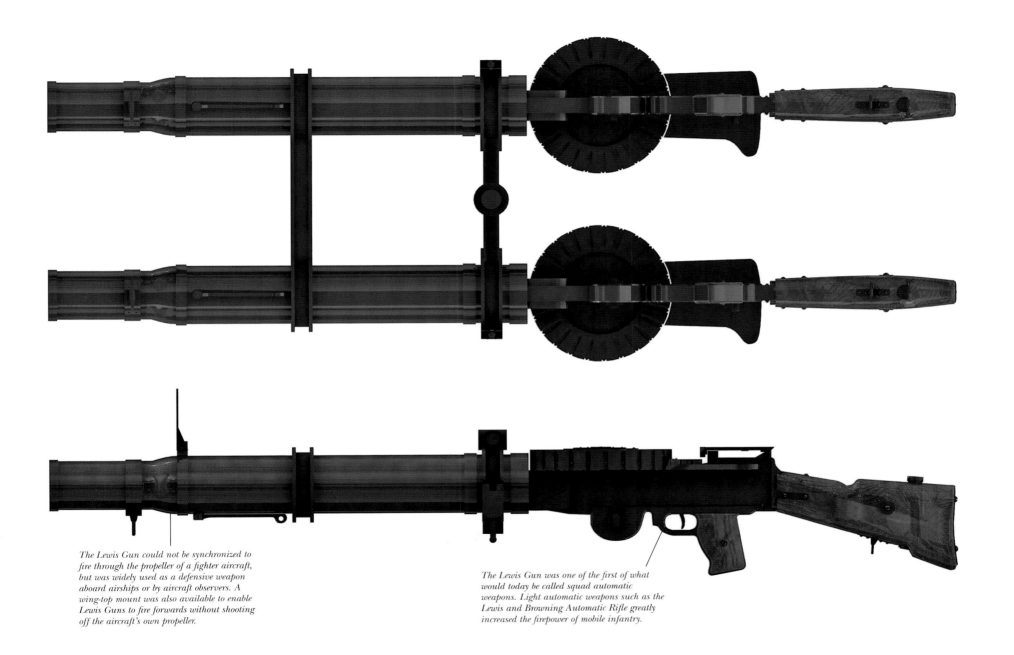

The Lewis Gun could not be synchronized to fire through the propeller of a fighter aircraft, but was widely used as a defensive weapon aboard airships or by aircraft observers. A wing-top mount was also available to enable Lewis Guns to fire forwards without shooting off the aircraft's own propeller.

The Lewis Gun was one of the first of what would today be called squad automatic weapons. Light automatic weapons such as the Lewis and Browning Automatic Rifle greatly increased the firepower of mobile infantry.

MOBILE FIRE SUPPORT

The Lewis Gun was often deployed in twin mounts for aircraft use, but these were simply a pair of weapons on a single mounting. On the ground, the Lewis Gun was light enough to be carried with advancing troops. This fulfilled a need for mobile fire support and assisted assault troops in holding and consolidating their gains in the face of a counterattack. The immediate aftermath of an assault was an ideal time to dislodge the enemy, while their forces were still weakened and disorganized, and before bulky medium machineguns could be brought forward to reinforce them. The Lewis Gun could also be used in the conventional defensive role, though there it was perhaps outshone by belt-fed, water-cooled weapons.

Browning .30 cal

The Browning '30-cal' family of machineguns began with the M1917, a water-cooled weapon that was primarily useful in the defensive role. Rugged and reliable, this weapon served through World War II even though it had been superseded by more advanced weapons. The Browning M1919 dispensed with the water jacket of the M1917 in favour of a perforated barrel shroud. It was not significantly lighter, however, and required a tripod or other fixed mount to operate; many were installed in US armoured vehicles. The M1919 weapon then went through a process of evolution, with several variants appearing. The A1, A2 and A3 models were lighter versions of the original M1919, developed in part so that mounted cavalry units could benefit from machinegun support. The definitive M1919 variant was the A4, which was adopted in the 1930s by all arms of the US military. With slight variations, it served as the standard support weapon aboard vehicles and in infantry formations until replacement by the M60 began in the 1960s. Examples are still in service in many nations. The M1919A5 was a slightly modified version for use aboard armoured vehicles and differed little from the A4 model. An attempt to modify the M1919 for a more mobile role was not as successful, however. Mating a shoulder stock to the bulky receiver and adding a bipod and flash hider created the A6 variant. This was too heavy and bulky, and most were converted back to A4 configuration as soon as possible.

SPECIFICATIONS

COUNTRY OF ORIGIN:	United States
DATE:	1919
CALIBRE:	7.69mm (0.30in) Browning
WEIGHT:	14.05kg (31lb)
OPERATION:	Short recoil
BARREL LENGTH:	610mm (24in)
MUZZLE VELOCITY:	853m/sec (2800ft/sec)
FEED:	250-round fabric or metal-link belt

BROWNING .30 CAL FACTS:

- .30–06 calibre general-purpose machinegun
- Used in vehicle and ground roles, and aboard aircraft
- Examples still in service today

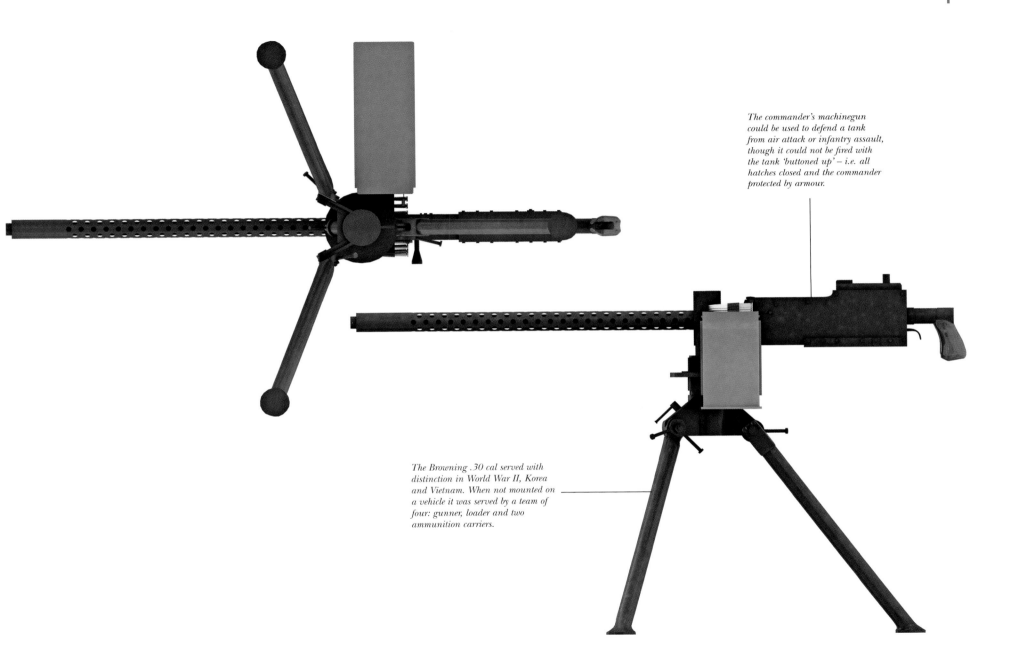

The commander's machinegun could be used to defend a tank from air attack or infantry assault, though it could not be fired with the tank 'buttoned up' – i.e. all hatches closed and the commander protected by armour.

The Browning .30 cal served with distinction in World War II, Korea and Vietnam. When not mounted on a vehicle it was served by a team of four: gunner, loader and two ammunition carriers.

A VERSATILE WEAPON

The Browning M1919 was a versatile weapon capable of fulfilling roles from infantry support to vehicle-mounted operations. Note the bipod retained on this tripod-mounted example; the same weapon could be switched from one role to another simply by changing the way it was mounted. The M1919's longevity as a weapon system stems from the fact that for many years there was no weapon that did any or all of its many jobs significantly better. It was, however, a weighty 'medium' machinegun and was eventually supplanted in the infantry support role by lighter general-purpose machineguns of the same general calibre. Bulk and weight are less significant in a vehicle-mounted weapon, so M1919s remained in service aboard tanks and personnel carriers for some time longer. Many were converted to NATO 7.62mm (0.3in) calibre.

M2 .50 cal

Experience in World War I caused senior US officers to request a heavy machinegun capable of engaging enemy armoured vehicles and aircraft. The weapon adopted to meet this need was designated M1921 and was essentially a water-cooled enlarged version of the Browning M1919. An improved air-cooled version was soon developed, designated M2. This weapon was given a heavier barrel to help dissipate heat built up in sustained firing. It thus became the M2HB (HB standing for heavy barrel) which is still in service today. The only major change that has been made since the 1930s is the introduction of quick-change barrels. The original design required careful adjustment after the barrel was attached to avoid a serious malfunction. The M2HB, except for some very recent models, had no manual safety catch. However, a bolt latch is fitted. This locks the bolt to the rear and must be released before firing. It can be used to fire single shots; the bolt is caught and locked after each round. M2s have been used as long-range sniping weapons in this manner. The M2 has a theoretical maximum range in excess of 7km (4.35 miles) but its effective range is less than 2km (1.24 miles). This is entirely sufficient for infantry support and light anti-aircraft work. M2s have seen service aboard aircraft and naval vessels as well as on land in vehicle or ground mounts. Versions have been built by several manufacturers and examples are in service worldwide.

SPECIFICATIONS

COUNTRY OF ORIGIN:	*United States*
DATE:	*1921*
CALIBRE:	*12.7mm (0.50in) BMG*
OPERATION:	*Short recoil*
WEIGHT:	*45.36kg (100lb)*
OVERALL LENGTH:	*1653mm (65in)*
BARREL LENGTH:	*1143mm (45in)*
MUZZLE VELOCITY:	*898m/sec (2950ft/sec)*
FEED:	*110-round metallic link belt*

M2 .50 CAL FACTS:

- .50 calibre air-cooled heavy machinegun
- Can be mounted on a tripod or a range of fixed mounts
- Can use armour-piercing ammunition

The M2 uses a distinctive 'spade handle' grip, until recently paired with a thumb-operated butterfly trigger. This could be made safe by inserting a spent cartridge behind the trigger, preventing it from being depressed. Some more recent models use squeeze triggers.

The M2 has served extensively as an air defence weapon in single, dual or quad mounts, and in a general role aboard many different vehicles. The usual mounting in this case is a single weapon on a pintle mount.

A HEAVY CONTENDER

The M2 lies at the upper end of the infantry weapons scale. It is far too big and heavy to be rapidly moved, unless it is mounted on a vehicle. In tripod-mounted configuration, it is normally used to defend strongpoints or bunkers, or positioned to provide fire support at medium to long ranges. Its large, high-velocity rounds can punch through many obstructions and can endanger aircraft and even light armoured vehicles, though no machinegun can hope to take on a main battle tank. The M2's resemblance to the Browning '.30-cal' M1919 is not coincidental; it is a scaled-up version of the same weapon. There are more modern heavy machineguns of course, but the M2 does its job well, and thus far there has been no need to replace it.

Bren MG

The Bren light machinegun got its name from the town of Brno in Czechoslovakia and Enfield in Britain. It was originally a Czech-developed weapon that was adopted, with some modifications, for service with the British army. Its top-loaded, downward-ejecting configuration was unusual but worked very well. The original prototype had a 20-round magazine, but the production model used a 30-round magazine and incorporated a mechanism for reducing felt recoil. The rate of fire was also reduced during development, eventually creating a weapon capable of highly accurate fire at a cyclic rate of 500rpm. The Bren Mk1 entered mass production in 1937, and was followed by a series of improved models over the next few years. The Mk1 could use a 100-round pan feed device, but later models could not. Most models incorporated fairly small changes, usually to make the weapon lighter or simpler to manufacture. The Bren served throughout World War II and long afterward. Those in British service were converted from the original .303 to 7.62 x 51mm (0.3 x 2in) NATO calibre, and designated L4. The last L4s were still in service in the 1980s. Other examples were exported to China and elsewhere. The Bren was primarily an infantry weapon, though it could be used aboard vehicles or in the anti-aircraft role. With a tripod and regular changes of barrel, it could undertake sustained fire, but its firepower was limited by being magazine rather than belt fed.

SPECIFICATIONS

COUNTRY OF ORIGIN:	United Kingdom/ Czechoslovakia
DATE:	1938
CALIBRE:	7.69mm (0.303in)
OPERATION:	Gas, air-cooled
WEIGHT:	10.25kg (22.5in)
OVERALL LENGTH:	1150mm (45.25in)
BARREL LENGTH:	625mm (25in)
MUZZLE VELOCITY:	730m/sec (2400ft/sec)
FEED:	30-round detachable box magazine

BREN MG FACTS:

- 0.303 (later 7.62 x 51mm/0.3 x 2in) light machinegun
- Top-mounted 30-round magazine
- Barrel changes necessary every 300 rounds under sustained fire

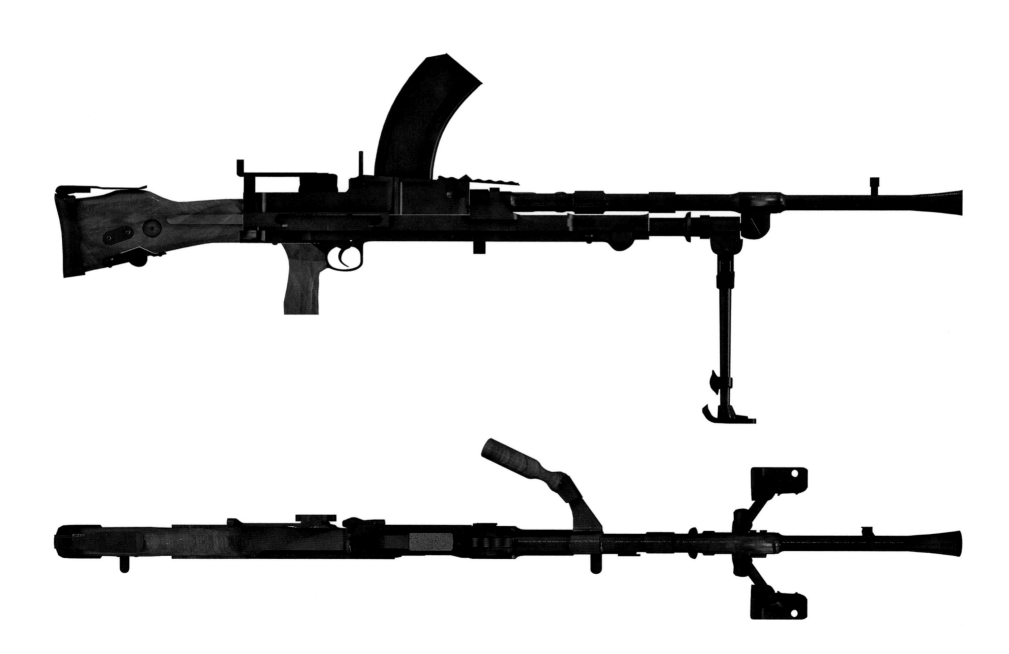

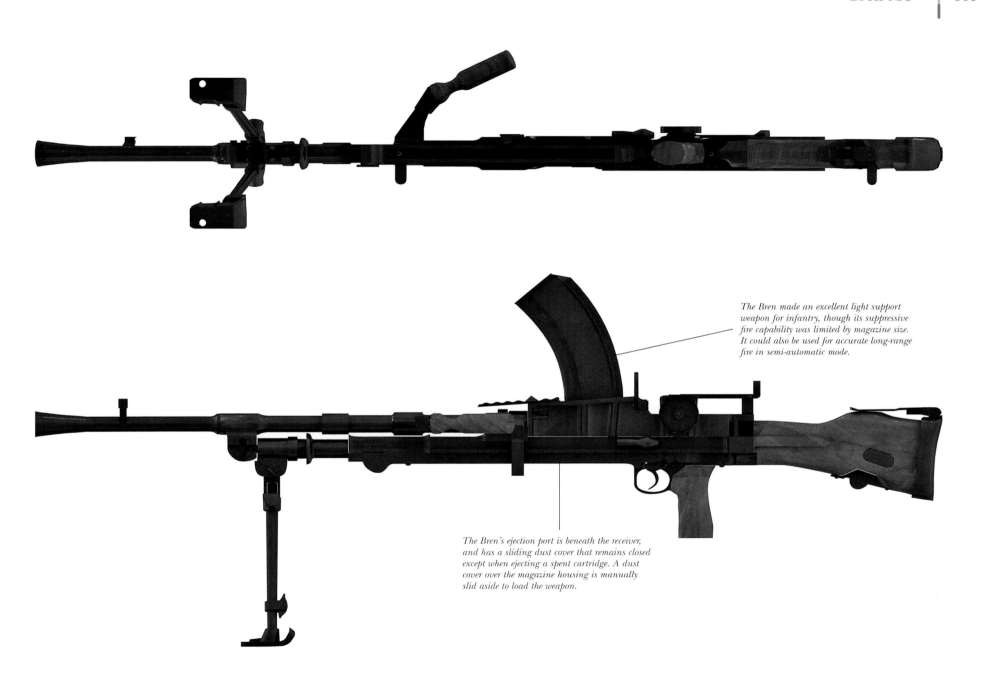

The Bren made an excellent light support weapon for infantry, though its suppressive fire capability was limited by magazine size. It could also be used for accurate long-range fire in semi-automatic mode.

The Bren's ejection port is beneath the receiver, and has a sliding dust cover that remains closed except when ejecting a spent cartridge. A dust cover over the magazine housing is manually slid aside to load the weapon.

PASSED INTO RESERVE

The Bren survived the changeover to 7.62 x 51mm (0.3 x 2in) ammunition but gradually passed from front-line use into reserve units. L4 Brens were issued to the RAF Regiment for airfield defence and to the navy for use when the occasion demanded it; they were also used on pintle mounts to arm vehicles. Some remained in storage and resurfaced from time to time, in much the same way that large numbers of L7 GPMGs reappeared in time for the 1991 Gulf War. By 1991 the L7 had, like the Bren, been supplanted in service by a newer weapon. However, some army units held onto guns that were well-respected by their users even if the policymakers had decided to get rid of them.

MG42

The concept of the general-purpose machinegun was arguably invented in Germany in the interwar years. Forbidden by the Treaty of Versailles from possessing heavy machineguns, the German armed forces sought a substitute. Work on this weapon was also outlawed by the treaty, but this did not prevent the creation of a rifle-calibre automatic weapon at plants in Switzerland and Austria. Designated MG30, this weapon was developed into the expensive and complex but highly effective MG34. Further development led to a simplified version designated MG42, which gradually replaced its predecessor in service during World War II. Although produced relatively quickly from cheap stamped metal components, the MG42 earned a solid reputation for reliability even under harsh conditions. The weapon's straight-through design reduced muzzle climb, and its ability to be used from a bipod, tripod or vehicle mount granted enormous versatility. The MG42 was chiefly notable for its extremely high rate of fire and distinctive sound, which earned it a variety of grim nicknames such as 'Hitler's Saw' and 'Bonesaw'. This in turn led to a need for a quick-change barrel to prevent overheating. Production of the MG42 was curtailed at the end of the war, but as soon as the West German Army was reconstituted it selected the MG42 as its light support weapon. Updated and redesignated first MG1 and later MG3, it continued to serve for many years. Versions were also adopted by the Austrian and Italian armed forces.

SPECIFICATIONS

COUNTRY OF ORIGIN:	Germany
DATE:	1942
CALIBRE:	7.92 x 57mm (0.31 x 2.24in) Mauser
OPERATION:	Short recoil
WEIGHT:	11.5kg (25lb 5oz)
OVERALL LENGTH:	1220mm (48in)
BARREL LENGTH:	535mm (21in)
MUZZLE VELOCITY:	800m/sec (2650ft/sec)
FEED:	50-round belt

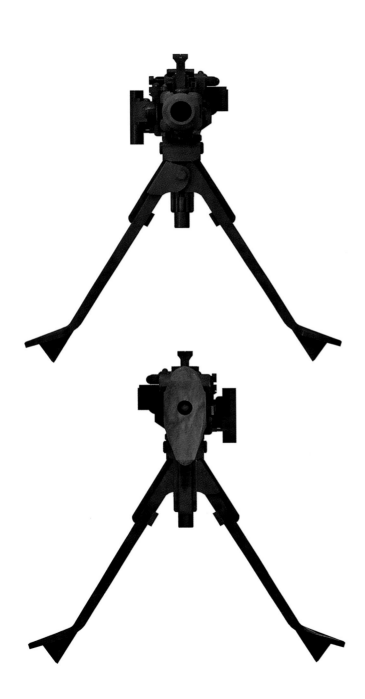

MG42 FACTS:

- 7.92 x 57mm (0.31 x 2.24in) calibre general-purpose machinegun
- Extremely high rate of fire
- Extremely resistant to dirt and dust

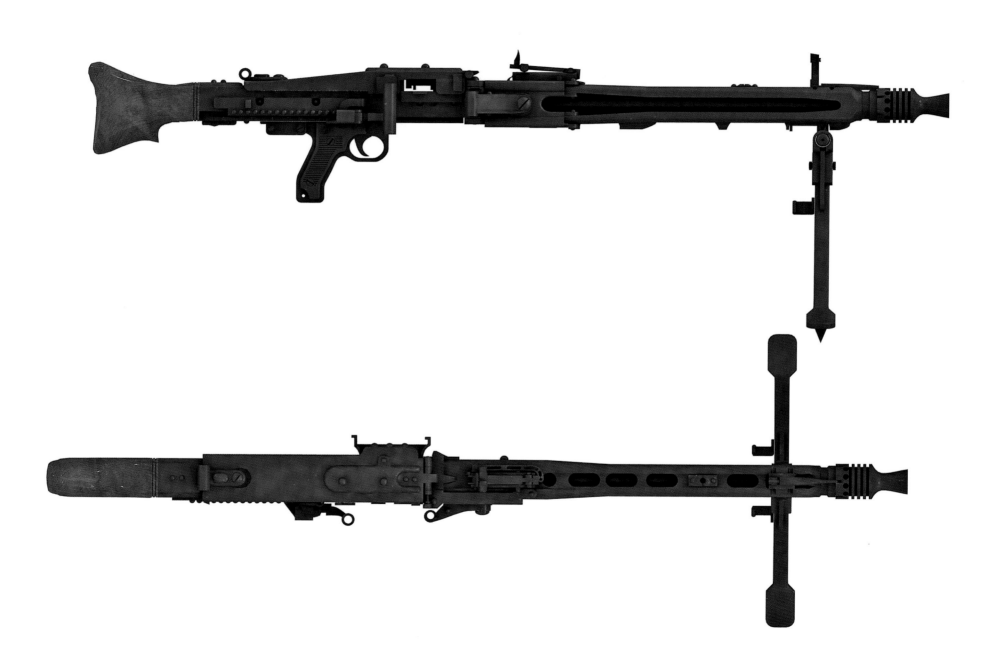

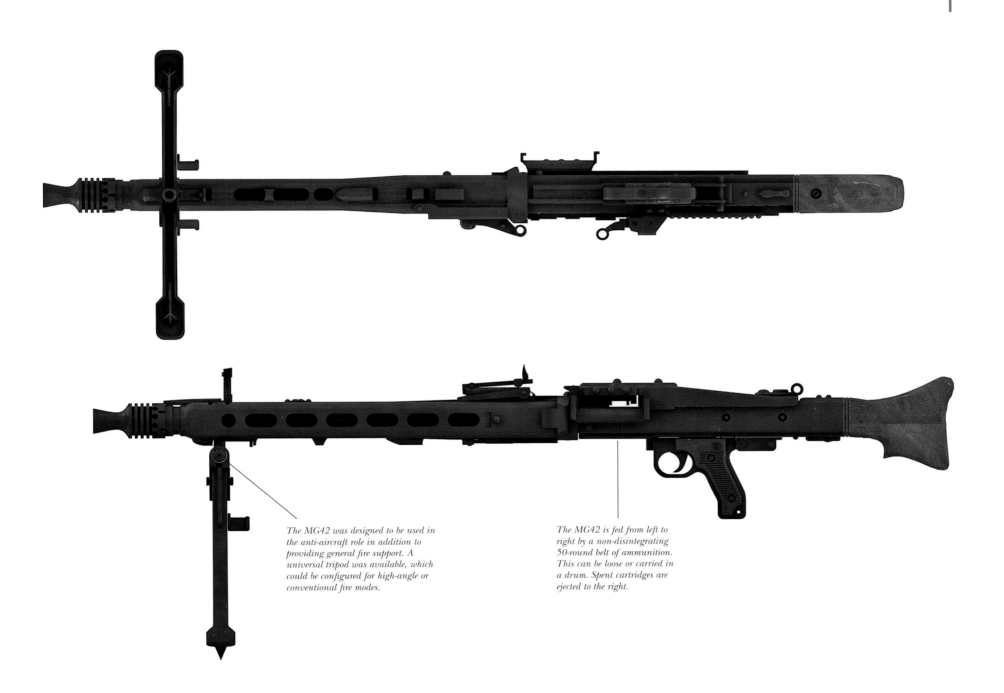

The MG42 was designed to be used in the anti-aircraft role in addition to providing general fire support. A universal tripod was available, which could be configured for high-angle or conventional fire modes.

The MG42 is fed from left to right by a non-disintegrating 50-round belt of ammunition. This can be loose or carried in a drum. Spent cartridges are ejected to the right.

REDUCING COSTS

The chief advantage of a general-purpose machinegun is its versatility. While it might not be the ideal weapon for every circumstance, a GPMG provides automatic fire wherever it is needed and is mobile enough to be taken wherever the troops go without slowing them down. Using the same weapon for many applications reduces costs and logistics burdens, making it easier to ensure that spares and replacements are available wherever they are needed. This in turn allows an army to save money to be spent on other things – or perhaps on more GPMGs. The MG42, and its predecessor, the MG34, were sufficiently effective in the general support role that similar weapons are still in use today.

M60

Experiments with German machineguns resulted in a mating of features from the FG42 and MG42, both of which were fine weapons. Unfortunately, the resulting early-model M60 was simply not as good as either of its parents. Most notable of the M60's failings was its barrel change: with no handle to hold the hot barrel by, changing one in action required an asbestos glove – which was easily lost. Since the barrel was an integral unit with bipod and gas cylinder, it was not only heavy and expensive but also robbed the weapon of support once it was removed. Other problems included the ability of the gas piston to be fitted backwards, preventing the weapon from using gas pressure to automatically reload itself, and a tendency of the gas block to dismantle itself under the vibration of firing. Later models ironed out most of the M60's faults, resulting in a more reliable weapon. The M60 can be mounted on a tripod or vehicle mount, or fired on the move. It has an integral bipod for mobile infantry support. A number of variants have appeared, including lightweight models and a version specifically designed to be mounted on a vehicle. The M60E3, was used with the US Marine Corps, had an 'assault' foregrip and could be used with a full-sized barrel for sustained fire support or a shorter assault barrel.

SPECIFICATIONS

COUNTRY OF ORIGIN:	United States
DATE:	1957
CALIBRE:	7.62mm (0.308in)
OPERATION:	Gas-operated, open bolt
WEIGHT:	10.5kg (23lb 2oz)
OVERALL LENGTH:	1105mm (43.5in)
BARREL LENGTH:	560mm (22in)
MUZZLE VELOCITY:	853m/sec (2800ft/sec)
FEED:	100– or 200–round metallic link belts

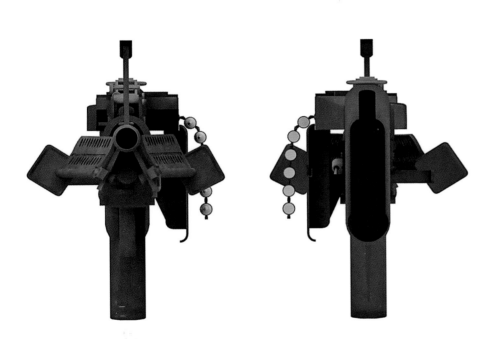

M60 FACTS:

● 7.62 x 51mm (0.3 x 2in) calibre general-purpose machinegun
● Modern versions are greatly improved over the original
● Fed from 100- or 200-round belts

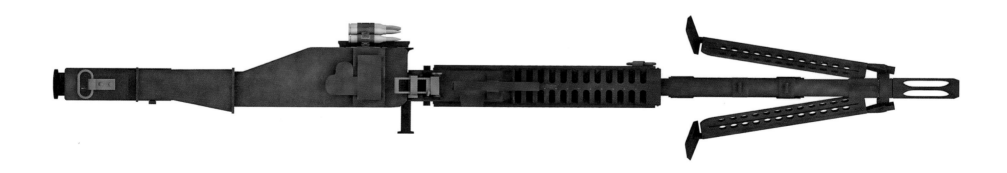

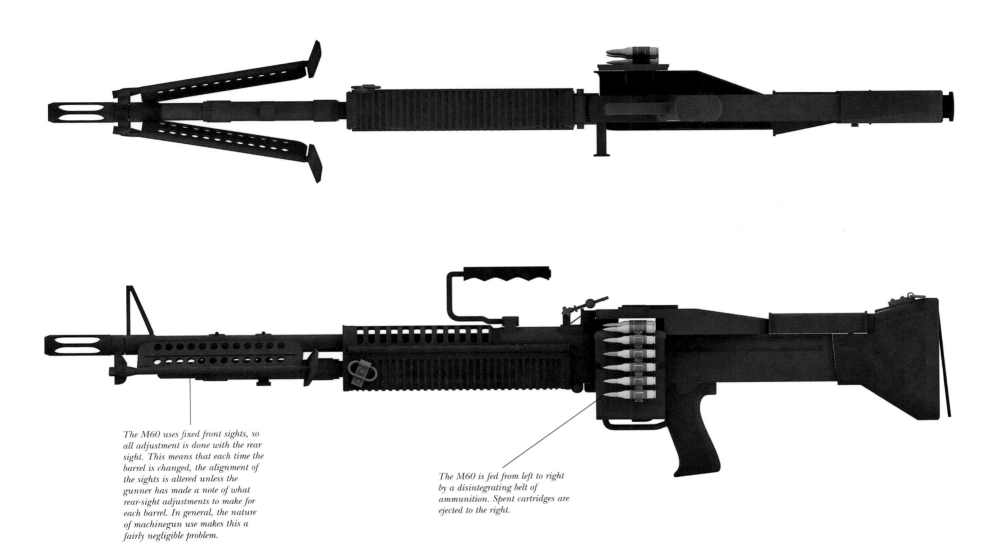

The M60 uses fixed front sights, so all adjustment is done with the rear sight. This means that each time the barrel is changed, the alignment of the sights is altered unless the gunner has made a note of what rear-sight adjustments to make for each barrel. In general, the nature of machinegun use makes this a fairly negligible problem.

The M60 is fed from left to right by a disintegrating belt of ammunition. Spent cartridges are ejected to the right.

ESSENTIAL TRAINING

Modern infantry training makes extensive use of low-powered lasers to simulate gunfire, along with blank rounds for authenticity. No training can ever be 100 per cent realistic, of course, but the closer to reality that training can get, the more effective it is. One of the most important aspects of infantry training is the psychological dimension, preparing soldiers to cope under the extreme stress of combat. No matter how good a marksman or gunner a soldier is, his skills are worthless if he panics under fire. The simplest of tasks, like loading a new belt into an M60, must be practised over and over in stressful conditions, until the task can be accomplished without conscious thought.

Bazooka

The weapon that became popularly known as the Bazooka was developed to meet the need of infantry for a close-range anti-tank weapon. Experiments with rocket-propelled rifle grenades led to a tube-shaped launcher that resembled the bazooka, a homemade musical instrument used by a popular comedian of the time. Although designated M9 Rocket Launcher, the new weapon was more widely known by its nickname. It fired a 59.94mm (2.36in) rocket that could, under the right conditions, penetrate a tank's armour. This required firing from a fairly close range, and the nature of the weapon was such that the crew were exposed to return fire during their attack. It was most effective in close-range urban fighting. Improved rocket design improved the M9's distinctly marginal performance, and work was underway on an improved version at the end of World War II. This weapon, the M20 Super Bazooka, became available during the Korean conflict. Unlike its predecessor, whose projectiles bounced off the North Korean T-34 tanks, the M20 was especially effective against tanks operating in urban terrain without infantry support. The Super Bazooka was used extensively during the Vietnam War, even though the enemy had few armoured vehicles. Its primary use was as a direct-fire support weapon to engage enemy bunkers or dug-in positions. Bazookas were gradually replaced by the M72 light anti-tank weapon during this period. Although not reusable, the M72 was sufficiently light that an infantryman could carry one in addition to his other kit.

SPECIFICATIONS

COUNTRY OF ORIGIN:	*United States*
DATE:	*1942*
CALIBRE:	*60mm (2.36in)*
LAUNCHER LENGTH:	*1545mm (61in)*
ROCKET TYPE:	*Shaped charge; 1.54kg (3lb 6oz)*
EFFECTIVE RANGE:	*137m (449.5ft)*
MAXIMUM RANGE:	*640m (2010ft)*
WEIGHT:	*5.98kg (13lb 2oz)*
MUZZLE VELOCITY:	*83m/sec (270ft/sec)*

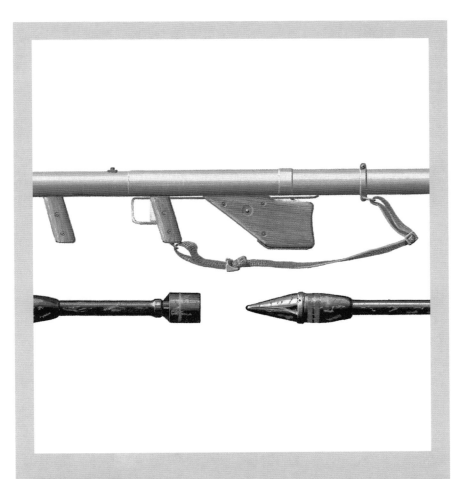

BAZOOKA FACTS:

- 59.94mm/2.36in (later 88.9mm/3.5in) calibre reusable anti-armour weapon
- Heavy and bulky
- Short effective range

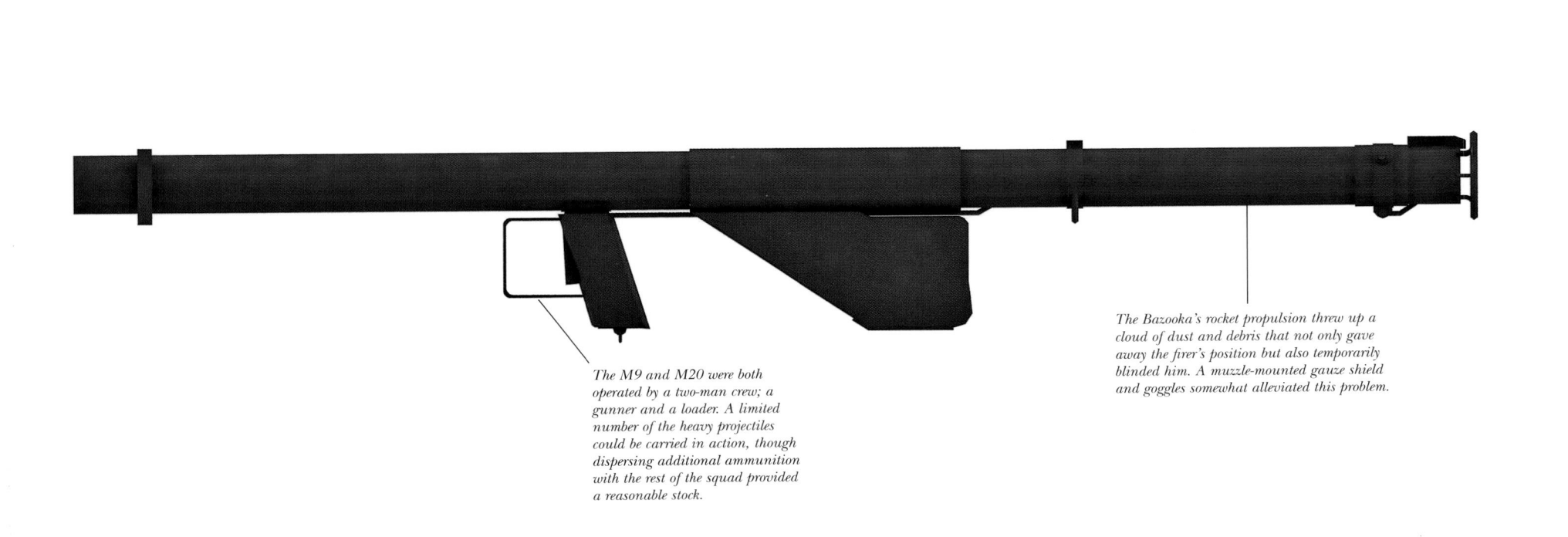

The M9 and M20 were both
operated by a two-man crew; a
gunner and a loader. A limited
number of the heavy projectiles
could be carried in action, though
dispersing additional ammunition
with the rest of the squad provided
a reasonable stock.

The Bazooka's rocket propulsion threw up a
cloud of dust and debris that not only gave
away the firer's position but also temporarily
blinded him. A muzzle-mounted gauze shield
and goggles somewhat alleviated this problem.

AVOIDING DEFEAT

Some military analysts have put forward the thesis that 'If you can't fight tanks, you can't fight'. Certainly the light anti-tank weapon has become an important part of the infantry support package, along with heavy machineguns such as the Browning M2. The Bazooka did not enable infantry to become deadly tank-hunters, but it did help infantry forces resist a tank attack and avoid being overrun. Bazookas were effective only at short range and could not penetrate the frontal armour of many tanks. Thus they were most useful when an enemy tank force had penetrated the infantry unit and bypassed some of its personnel. In this role, it was a weapon for avoiding defeat rather than winning battles against tanks – that job went to the big guns of friendly armoured vehicles.

Panzerfaust

The Panzerfaust was a cheap, disposable anti-tank weapon, the forerunner of today's Light Anti-tank Weapons (LAW) and rocket-propelled grenade launchers such as the RPG-7. It consisted of a shaped-charge projectile and a tube-shaped launcher. The latter contained gunpowder as a propellant and mounted a rather crude aiming device. The weapon was aimed by unfolding the sighting device and looking at the target through a hole marked for the appropriate range – 30, 60, 80 or 150m (98, 197, 263 or 492ft). When the trigger was operated, a percussion device struck sparks to ignite the powder. This resulted in a very significant backblast that could endanger personnel behind the firer and would certainly give away his position. After firing, the launch tube was discarded. The shaped-charge warhead was able to penetrate most tanks of the World War II period. It did not rely on impacting at high velocity like the anti-tank guns and anti-armour rifles of the period, but instead focused the hot gases generated by the exploding warhead into a jet that cut its way into the target. The weapon itself was extremely simple to use. It granted a measure of anti-armour capability to ordinary infantry squads without the need for a specialist weapon, and was widely issued to militia troops such as Hitler Youth members during the final defence of Berlin. A reloadable version, with a reusable launch tube, was eventually developed, though too late to have any real effect on the war.

SPECIFICATIONS

COUNTRY OF ORIGIN:	Germany
DATE:	1943
CALIBRE:	149mm (5.87in) (Panzerfaust 60)
LAUNCHER LENGTH:	762mm (30in)
EFFECTIVE RANGE:	60m (197ft)
WEIGHT:	6.8kg (15lb) total
MUZZLE VELOCITY:	45m/sec (148ft/sec)
ARMOUR PENETRATION:	200mm (7.87in)

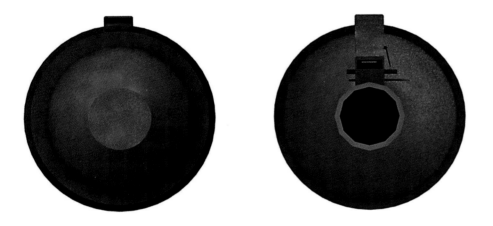

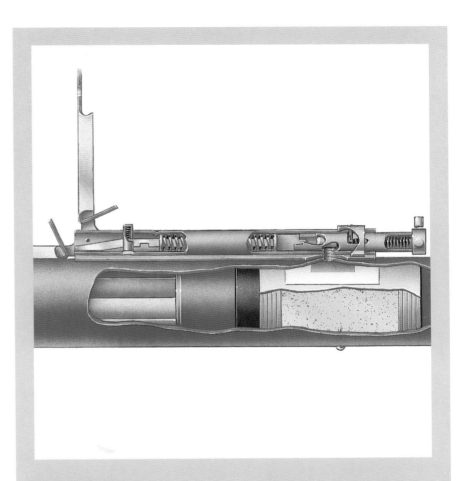

PANZERFAUST FACTS:

- Disposable anti-tank weapon
- Inaccurate at longer ranges
- Capable of penetrating most tanks of the time

In the last stages of World War II, many personnel were sent into action armed with nothing but a Panzerfaust.

The Panzerfaust was highly effective in close-quarters urban fighting, where infantry were able to remain concealed and ambush tanks from the side or rear.

MASS-PRODUCTION

The Panzerfaust was improved several times after its invention, but it remained a cheap and simple weapon that could be mass-produced for use by personnel who were virtually untrained. During the final defence of Germany, thousands of Panzerfausts were handed out to the Hitler Youth and other hastily-fielded forces. In the close terrain of a city, they were effective against tanks and also in attacks on groups of personnel. Although it was a weapon of desperation, the Panzerfaust inspired generations of light anti-tank weapons. It was the progenitor of both the Russian RPG-7 family and the disposable Light Anti-tank Weapon (LAW) used by Western forces.

RPG-7

The RPG-7 is a rocket-propelled grenade launcher initially developed as an anti-armour weapon but currently used in a more general support role as well. It consists of a reusable launcher and a rocket-propelled grenade that is launched by a gunpowder charge before igniting its rocket a safe distance from the firer. The calibre of the weapon is normally given as 40mm (1.58in), as this is the size of the launcher tube into which the tail of the grenade fits. Actual warhead diameter varies depending on the grenade type; it can be as much as 105mm (4.13in). The grenade is stabilized by fins in flight and has a theoretical indirect-fire maximum range of 920m (3018ft) depending on the grenade type. However, there is little chance of a direct hit at ranges much over 200–300m (656–984ft). The RPG-7 was introduced in the 1960s. The basic launcher has changed little, though a variety of sighting aids have become available. A range of improved warheads have also been developed. These include shaped-charge anti-armour, tandem anti-armour to defeat reactive armour, thermobaric (fuel-air explosive) and fragmentation payloads. A copy of the RPG-7, built by a US manufacturer, can also deliver less-lethal payloads such as tear gas. Despite improved warheads, this weapon is a somewhat marginal threat to a modern main battle tank. However, it is a cheap and effective means of providing infantry with area-effect support weapons and a measure of defence against tanks.

SPECIFICATIONS

COUNTRY OF ORIGIN:	USSR
DATE:	1961
CALIBRE:	40mm (1.57in) barrel, 85mm (3.35in) warhead
LAUNCHER LENGTH:	950mm (37.4in)
EFFECTIVE RANGE:	920m (3018ft) max
WEIGHT:	7kg (15lb)
MUZZLE VELOCITY:	114m/sec (374ft/sec)
ARMOUR PENETRATION:	330mm (13in)

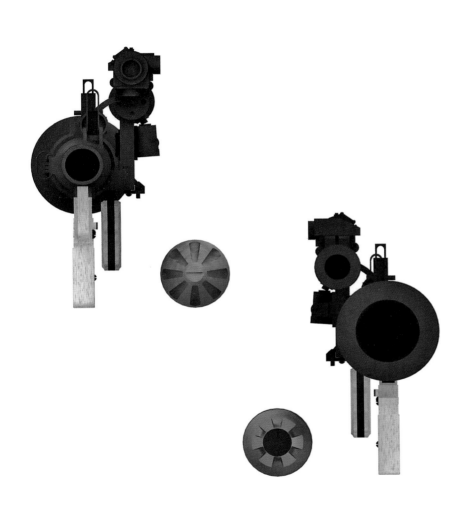

RPG-7 FACTS:

- Reusable anti-armour weapon
- Variety of warheads available
- Powered flight to about 500m (1640ft)

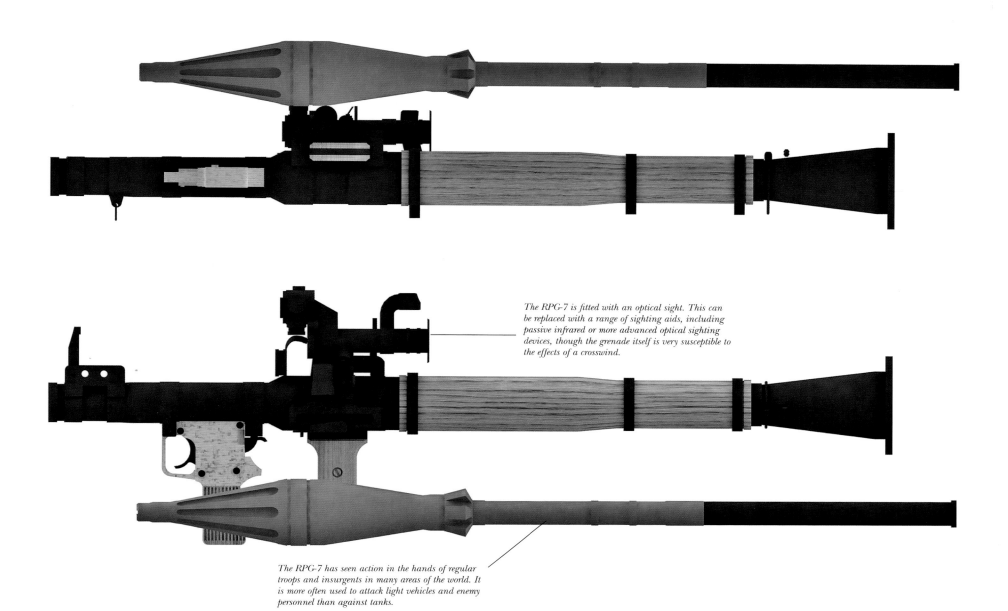

The RPG-7 is fitted with an optical sight. This can be replaced with a range of sighting aids, including passive infrared or more advanced optical sighting devices, though the grenade itself is very susceptible to the effects of a crosswind.

The RPG-7 has seen action in the hands of regular troops and insurgents in many areas of the world. It is more often used to attack light vehicles and enemy personnel than against tanks.

TEAM WORK

The rear part of the RPG-7 is a reusable launcher, into which the long tail of the grenade is fitted. The grenades themselves are sufficiently bulky that RPG gunners work as part of a team, with at least one other soldier carrying grenades. Other members of the squad may also have a grenade as part of their issued equipment. Although the RPG-7 has a nominal range of about 1000m (3280ft), a hit on a moving target is unlikely beyond 100–200m (328–656ft). At longer ranges, it is more or less pointless to shoot at a tank, but harassing fire against enemy infantry positions remains an option. As with other light antitank weapons, the RPG-7 is unlikely to disable a main battle tank but can be highly effective against armoured personnel carriers.

Stinger

The Stinger missile is best known as a shoulder-fired Man-Portable Air Defence System (MANPADS), but it can also be launched from a vehicle or helicopter-carried mount. It tracks its target using a passive infrared system, homing in on the target's heat sources. Once locked on the target, the weapon is self-guiding, allowing the user to reload and engage another target, or take cover, while the missile is in the air. The Stinger system consists of a reusable launch unit and a missile, which is contained within a disposable tube. The launch unit incorporates the sighting system and an IFF (Identification Friend-or-Foe) unit. This sends a coded radio pulse to the target and emits a tone if an authentic 'friendly' response comes back. A different tone indicates a non-friendly aircraft, or one not tied into the IFF system. The Stinger uses proportional guidance, which causes the missile to over-correct for the target's evasive manoeuvres. This increases the chances of a hit, and lethality is improved by the terminal guidance unit, which selects an aim point slightly away from the hottest part of the target. This biases the impact point towards the most vulnerable components of an aircraft. A number of variants and improved versions of the Stinger have been implemented. Some are electronic upgrades to the basic system, but others are more radical. Air-to-Air Stinger (ATAS) is designed for use aboard helicopters and unmanned air vehicles (UAVs). It was first demonstrated in 1996.

SPECIFICATIONS

COUNTRY OF ORIGIN:	United States
DATE:	1981
LENGTH:	1520mm (59.84in)
WEIGHT:	15.2kg (33lb 8oz)
WARHEAD WEIGHT:	3kg (6lb 10oz)
GUIDANCE SYSTEM:	Infrared homing

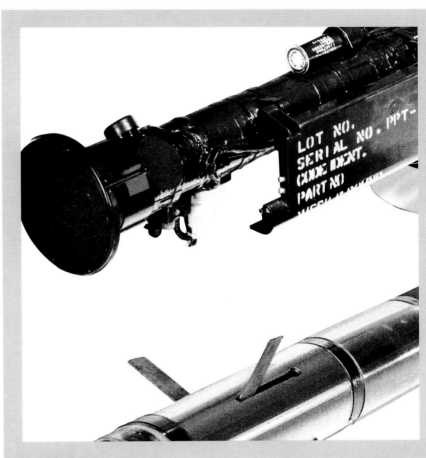

STINGER FACTS:

- Shoulder-fired anti-aircraft missile
- Passive infrared guidance
- Missile achieves supersonic speeds

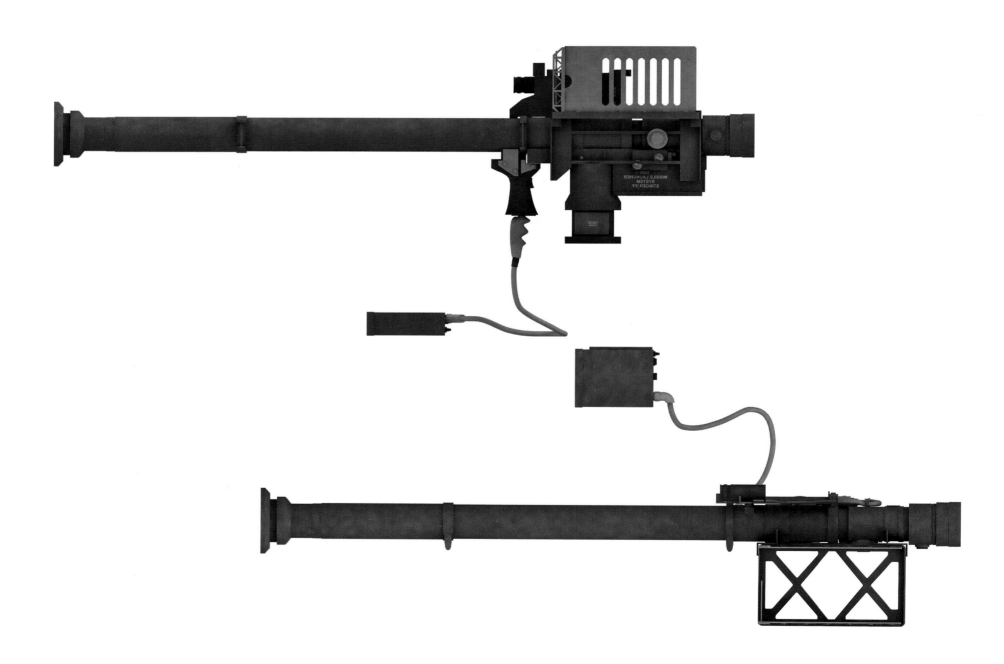

MISSILE LAUNCHER
SYSTEM
STINGER IFF

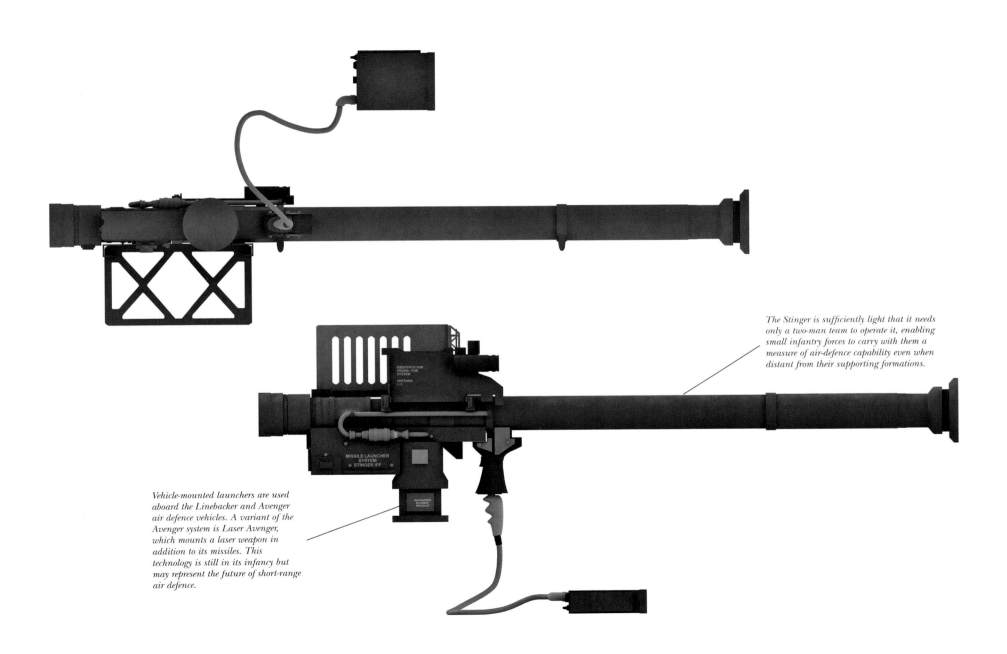

The Stinger is sufficiently light that it needs only a two-man team to operate it, enabling small infantry forces to carry with them a measure of air-defence capability even when distant from their supporting formations.

Vehicle-mounted launchers are used aboard the Linebacker and Avenger air defence vehicles. A variant of the Avenger system is Laser Avenger, which mounts a laser weapon in addition to its missiles. This technology is still in its infancy but may represent the future of short-range air defence.

FREQUENT UPDATES

The range of threats faced by infantry has increased over the last century to include armoured vehicles and aircraft. Small arms fire is unlikely to be much use against these threats, so specialist weapons are necessary. It is not possible to carry large numbers of anti-tank or anti-aircraft weapons, as they are very bulky. Thus for airborne threats it is necessary to create an effective counter that 'uses up' as few riflemen as possible. The Stinger and other weapons like it are continually updated to cope with advances in enemy countermeasures or tactics, and ideally to make the weapon lighter and less bulky. However, the latter rarely occurs – weapon systems have a tendency to become larger and more complex over time rather than the reverse.

Index

Page references in *italics* refer to illustration captions

A
AB-10 96, 101, *101 see also* Tec9
accuracy 7–8
AK47 132, *132*, 133, *133, 134, 135, 136–7*, 137
AKM 132
ammunition 7
    ACP (Automatic Colt Pistol), .45: 30, 35, 60, 72, 77
    AMP (Automag Pistol), .44: 42
    Dragunov 144
    Magnum, .44: 36
    Martini-Henry 120
    M16 143
    SIG .357 (9mm) 48
    StG44 126
anti-aircraft missile, Stinger 216, *216*, 217, *217, 218, 219, 220*, 221, *221*
anti-armour weapon, RPG-7 210, *210*, 211, *211, 212, 213, 214–15*, 215
anti-tank weapons
    bazooka 198, *198*, 199, *199, 200, 201, 202*, 203, *203*
    Panzerfaust 204, *204*, 205, *205, 206, 207, 208–9*, 209
Assault Weapons Ban, US (1996) 96, 101
Automag 180: 42, *42, 43, 43, 44, 45, 46–7*, 47

B
Barrett Firearms Company 150 *see also* M82 'Light Fifty; M107
barricade position *64–5*, 65
bazooka 198, *198*, 199, *199, 200, 201, 202*, 203, *203*
Beretta 92: 48, 53

Beretta 93R (Raffica) 54, *54*, 55, *55, 56, 57*, 58, *58, 59*
Borchardt, Hugo 24
Bren MG *9*, 180, *180*, 181, *181, 182, 183, 184*, 185, *185*
British forces 162
    army 120
    naval infantry *124–5*, 125
Browning, John 30, 48
Browning .30 cal 168, *168*, 169, *169, 170, 171, 172–3*, 173
Browning M1919 .30 cal 168, *172–3*, 173

C
carbines 8, 156
    KAR-98k 108
    M4A1 156, *156*, 157, *157, 158, 159, 160–1*, 161
categories 8–9
Colt M1911 30, *30*, 31, *31, 32, 33, 34*, 35, *35*

D
dog lock pistol 12, *12*, 13, *13, 14, 15, 16, 17*
Dragunov SVD 144, *144*, 145, *145, 146, 147, 148–9*, 149
Dragunov SVD-S 144

F
flintlock *see* dog lock pistol

G
G98 108
Gal, Uziel 84
Galil 132
German Army, West 186
grenade launchers
    M203 138, *138*, 139, *139, 140, 141*
    RPG-7 rocket-propelled 210, *210*, 211, *211, 212, 213, 214–15*, 215
Gulf War 150

H
Hathcock, Carlos 114, 119
Heckler & Koch MP5 90, *94–5*, 95 *see also* MP5K
Henry, Alexander 120
Hitler Youth 204, 209

I
infantry force equipment 9
Intratec 96
Israeli military 84

K
Kalashnikov 132 *see also* AK47
KAR-98 108, *108*, 109, *109, 110, 111, 112*, 113, *113*
KAR-98k 108

L
Lee, J.P. 102
Lee-Enfield 102, *102*, 103, *103, 104, 105, 106–7*, 107
Lee-Metford 102, 120
Lewis, Isaac Newton 162
Lewis Gun 162, *162*, 163, *163, 164, 165, 166–7*, 167
'Light Fifty', M82 150, *150*, 151, *151, 152, 153, 154*, 155, *155*
Luger, George 24
Luger (Parabellum (P) '08) 24, *24*, 25, *25, 26, 27, 28–9*, 29

M
M1 SMG 72 *see also* Thompson M1928
M2 .50 cal 174, *174*, 175, *175, 176, 177, 178*, 179, *179*
M4A1 156, *156*, 157, *157, 158, 159, 160–1*, 161
M9 Rocket Launcher 198, *198*, 199, *199, 200, 201, 202*, 203, *203*
M16 138, 143

M16A1/A2 138, *138*, 139, *139*, *140*, *141*, *142–3*, 143

M20 Super Bazooka 198, *201*

M40 (Remington 700) *117*

M60 192, *192*, 193, *193*, *194*, *195*, *196*, 197, *197*

M72 light anti-tank weapon 198

M82 'Light Fifty' 150, *150*, 151, *151*, *152*, *153*, *154*, 155, *155*

M107 150, *150*, 151, *151*, *152*, *153*, *154*, 155, *155*

M203 grenade launcher 138, *138*, 139, *139*, *140*, *141*

machineguns 9
  Bren light 9, 180, *180*, 181, *181*, *182*, *183*, *184*, 185, *185*
  Browning .30 cal 168, *168*, 169, *169*, *170*, *171*, *172–3*, 173
  Browning M1919 .30 cal 168, *172–3*, 173
  Lewis light 162, *162*, 163, *163*, *164*, *165*, *166–7*, 167
  M2 .50 cal heavy 174, *174*, 175, *175*, *176*, *177*, *178*, 179, *179*
  M60 192, *192*, 193, *193*, *194*, *195*, *196*, 197, *197*
  MG34 186
  MG42 186, *186*, 187, *187*, *188*, *189*, *190*, *191*

Magnum, .44 *see* Smith & Wesson M29

'Magnum flinch' 41

MANPADS (Man-Portable Air Defence System) *see* Stinger

Marskmen, Designated 144, 149

Martini, Frederich 120

Martini-Henry 120, *120*, 121, *121*, *122*, *123*, *124–5*, 125

Mauser G98 108

Metford, W.E. 102

MG34 186

MG42 186, *186*, 187, *187*, *188*, *189*, *190*, *191*

missile, Stinger anti-aircraft 216, *216*, 217, *217*, *218*, *219*, *220*, *221*

MP5K 90, *90*, 91, *91*, *92*, *93 see also* Heckler & Koch MP5

MP38 66, *66*, 67, *67*, *68*, *69*, *70*, 71, *71*

MP40 66, 71

MP44 *see* StG44

N

naval infantry, British *124–5*, 125

P

Panzerfaust 204, *204*, 205, *205*, *206*, *207*, *208–9*, 209

Parabellum '08 *see* Luger

pepperbox .45: 18, *18*, 19, *19*, *20*, *21*, *22–3*, 23

percussion cap 18

pistols 17 *see also* revolvers
  Automag 180: 42, *42*, 43, *43*, *44*, *45*, *46–7*, 47
  Beretta 93R (Raffica) 54, *54*, 55, *55*, *56*, *57*, 58, *58*, *59*
  Colt M1911 30, *30*, 31, *31*, *32*, *33*, *34*, 35, *35*
  dog lock 12, *12*, 13, *13*, *14*, *15*, *16*, 17
  Luger (Parabellum (P) '08) 24, *24*, 25, *25*, *26*, *27*, *28–9*, 29
  pepperbox .45: 18, *18*, 19, *19*, *20*, *21*, *22–3*, 23
  SIG-Sauer P226 48, *48*, 49, *49*, *50*, *51*, *52*, 53, *53*
  Smith & Wesson 4506 60, *60*, 61, *61*, *62*, *63*, *64–5*

R

rails, Picatinny *159*, *160–1*, 161

Remington 700 (M40) *117 see also* Winchester M70

revolvers 36
  Smith & Wesson M29 (.44 Magnum) *6*, 36, *36*, 37, *37*, *38*, *39*, *40–1*, 41

rifles 8
  Dragunov SVD 144, *144*, 145, *145*, *146*, *147*, *148–9*, 149
  Dragunov SVD-S 144

G98 108

Galil 132

KAR-98 108, *108*, 109, *109*, *110*, *111*, *112*, 113, *113*

Lee-Enfield 102, *102*, 103, *103*, *104*, *105*, *106–7*, 107

Lee-Metford 102, 120

M82 'Light Fifty' 150, *150*, 151, *151*, *152*, *153*, *154*, 155, *155*

M107 150, *150*, 151, *151*, *152*, *153*, *154*, 155, *155*

Martini-Henry 120, *120*, 121, *121*, *122*, *123*, *124–5*, 125

Valmet 132

Winchester M70 *8*, 114, *114*, 115, *115*, *116*, *117*, *118–19*, 119

rifles, anti-materiel 150, 155 *see also* M82 'Light Fifty'; M107

rifles, assault 9
  AK47 132, *132*, 133, *133*, *134*, *135*, *136–7*, 137
  AKM 132
  M16 138, 143
  M16A1/A2 138, *138*, 139, *139*, *140*, *141*, *142–3*, 143
  StG44 (Sturmgewehr-44) 126, *126*, 127, *127*, *128*, *129*, *130–1*, 131

Rocket Launcher, M9 198, *198*, 199, *199*, *200*, *201*, 202, 203, *203*

Royal Navy, infantry *124–5*, 125

RPG-7 210, *210*, 211, *211*, *212*, *213*, *214–15*, 215

S

SIG-Sauer P226 48, *48*, 49, *49*, *50*, *51*, *52*, 53, *53*

Smith & Wesson 4506 60, *60*, 61, *61*, *62*, *63*, *64–5*

Smith & Wesson M29 (.44 Magnum) *6*, 36, *36*, 37, *37*, *38*, *39*, *40–1*, 41

SMLE (Short Magazine Lee-Enfield) 102, *105 see also* Lee-Enfield

snipers 113, *113*, 114, *118–19*, 119, 144, 150

Sten Mk II 78, *78*, 79, *79*, *80*, *81*, 83
Sten Mk IIS ('Silent Sten') 78, *82–3*, 83
StG44 *see* Sturmgewehr-44
Stinger 216, *216*, 217, *217*, *218*, *219*, 220, 221, *221*
'stopping power' 6–7
Sturmgewehr-44 (StG44) 126, *126*, 127, *127*, *128*, *129*, *130–1*, 131
submachineguns 8, 66, 71, 72
    AB-10 96, 101, *101 see also* Tec9
    Heckler & Koch MP5 90, *94–5*, 95 *see also* MP5K
    MP5K 90, *90*, 91, *91*, *92*, *93 see also* Heckler & Koch MP5
    MP38 66, *66*, 67, *67*, *68*, *69*, *70*, 71, *71*
    Sten Mk II 78, *78*, 79, *79*, *80*, *81*, 83
    Sten Mk IIS ('Silent Sten') 78, *82–3*, 83
    Tec9 (TEC-DC9) 7, 96, *96*, 97, *97*, *98*, *99*, *100*, 101 *see also* AB-10
    Thompson M1928 72, *72*, 73, *73*, *74*, *75*, *76–7*, 77, 96
    Uzi 84, *84*, 85, *85*, *86*, *87*, *88–9*, 89
Super Bazooka, M20 198, *201*
support weapons 9
SVD *see* Dragunov SVD
Swiss army 24

T
Tec9 (TEC-DC9) 7, 96, *96*, 97, *97*, *98*, *99*, *100*, 101 *see also* AB-10
Thompson, John T. 72
Thompson M1928 72, *72*, 73, *73*, *74*, *75*, *76–7*, 77, 96
training, infantry 197

U
US Marine Corps 156, 192
Uzi 84, *84*, 85, *85*, *86*, *87*, *88–9*, 89

V
Valmet 132
Versailles, Treaty of 186
Vietnam War 114, *118–19*, 119, 143, 150, 198

W
Winchester M70 *8*, 114, *114*, 115, *115*, *116*, *117*, *118–19*, 119
World War I *107*

Picture Credits

All Artworks © Military Visualizations, Inc. (www.milviz.com)

Photographs:

Alamy: 28/29 (B. Christopher), 40/41 (Woody Stock), 53 (Andrew Chittock), 94/95 (Altered Images)

Art-Tech/Aerospace: 46/47, 58, 67, 73, 79, 85, 103, 109, 127, 151, 163, 169, 175, 181, 187, 193, 199, 205

Art-Tech/John Batchelor: 13, 19, 37

Art-Tech/MARS: 13, 19, 37

Bridgeman: 16 (Look & Learn), 22/23 (Peter Newark)

Cody Images: 70, 71, 91, 112, 113, 118/119, 131, 137, 178, 179, 184, 185, 190, 191, 202, 203, 220, 221

Corbis: 59 (Gianni Giansanti/Sygma), 88/89 (David H. Wells), 97 (Ted Soqui)

Dorling Kindersley: 211

Dreamstime: 139 (RC Photo), 145 (Mariusz Lubkowski)

Mary Evans Picture Library: 130 (Suddeutscher Zeitung)

Getty Images: 100 (Marty Katz/Time & Life), 148/149 (AFP)

William Richard King (Kingsforgeandmuzzleloading.com): 17

Kobal: 65 (Warner Brothers)

Photos.com: 25, 31, 49, 121, 133, 157

Press Association: 101

Smith & Wesson: 61, 64

U. S. Department of Defense: 34, 35, 52, 136, 154, 155, 160/161, 196, 197, 217